SIMPLY DEVINE

To Joyce
With lots of love

SIMPLY DEVINE
The Sydney Devine Story

Sydney Devine
_x_

Sydney Devine
with
Matt Bendoris

BLACK & WHITE PUBLISHING

First published 2005
by Black & White Publishing Ltd
99 Giles Street, Edinburgh, EH6 6BZ

ISBN 1 84502 057 X

A CIP catalogue record for this book is available from the British Library.

Printed and bound by Creative Print and Design Group Ltd

CONTENTS

TO SHIRLEY, MY WIFE

Without you, this book would never have been written because there is no way my career could have been so successful if I had not met you. From the first time I saw you in the Tivoli Theatre in Aberdeen, my life changed for the better. Through the years, you have been my sweetheart, my lover, my wife, my lawyer, my secretary, my doctor, my financial advisor, my banker, my housekeeper, my chef, my tailor, my chauffeur, my shoulder to cry on and mother to our three children.

If, after all these years together, I haven't told you how much you mean to me, then please forgive me for not telling you before now. Just saying thank you seems inadequate – I could never praise your many talents highly enough. If I could give you the world, you would have it tomorrow – but, no doubt, you would start to clean it!

I love you,
Syd

INTRODUCTION

As I stood outside the gates of Buckingham Palace, my legs began to shake. It got a lot worse inside and my wife Shirley insists that I was trembling so much she could see my kilt move. Suddenly there she was before me – the Queen, speaking to me. I babbled something about meeting her before during her Silver Jubilee celebrations in 1977, at the King's Theatre in Glasgow, and the only words I can remember her saying were, 'My, that was a long time ago.' I'm sure she said something else after that but it was all just a blur – if my life depended on it, I couldn't recall another word she said to me that day.

I'm not quite sure when the tears began. I know I didn't cry in front of the Queen but I certainly felt like it and was convinced I was going to make a fool of myself and break down, right there, in front of Her Majesty. Outside I posed for the cameras with my MBE and I most definitely cried then. The papers loved it as they could roll out their 'Tiny Bubbles' headlines. I was asked if it had been nerves that had brought the tears to my eyes and they had certainly been a factor but it wasn't just that. I had been overwhelmed by the whole event, swept away on a tidal wave of emotion which had nothing to do with the grandeur of the special occasion. It was the fact that it had happened to *me* – a boy from the mining village of Bellside had ended up at Buckingham Palace – and it was also to do with the unbelievable journey I'd been on to get there . . .

1

THE EARLY YEARS

I was born on the 11th of January 1940, the youngest in a family of nine children – there was no television in those days so families were big. My dad Daniel was a brusher in a mine. A brusher, from what I can gather, was someone who cleaned a route to a new seam. He got rid of all the muck and filth on the pit floor and kept the road clear, so to speak. He was a hard worker and, as a young boy, I had to meet him at the bottom of the hill to push his bike home because he didn't have the energy to do it himself. He was a wonderful man, very passive. My father never lifted a hand to me in his life and was the same with all my brothers and sisters.

However, if there was ever any disciplining to be done, my mother did it, that's for sure. Luckily, in those early days of my youth, the beds were pretty high so you could hide under them right at the back against the wall and your mother could never get hold of you! My mother's name was Helen but she was better known as Old Nellie. Despite dishing out the discipline, she wasn't really that fearsome and, like many of the women back then, she really kept everything together. I think, if she hadn't been so organised, my father would have had to hire a sheep dog to round us all up.

Although I was born into a family of nine, only eight survived. The death of a sibling was common in those turbulent days but I wouldn't discover that this had happened to our family until much later in life. I still don't know whether it was a brother or sister who died. My oldest brother was Hughie (Hugh) and, after him, there was Agnes, George, Jean, Lorna, Danny, Andrew and then me. I don't know what the age difference between Hugh and me is – all I know is that we kids seemed to come along roughly every three years. There was three years between Andrew and me, three years between Andrew and Danny, then another three between Danny and my sister Lorna and so on.

I had a fantastic relationship with them all – with the exception of my nearest brother who, bearing in mind that he had been the baby until I came along, was naturally jealous. But, as was the case in most big families, the sisters helped raise the kids and seemingly Agnes more or less brought me up. When I went to school, I told the teacher that I had two mammies – a 'mammy mammy' and an 'Agnes mammy' – and I always remember my teacher thinking this was rather peculiar.

Home was the village of Bellside which, as I always say, was a 'suburb' of Cleland, one of many thriving mining communities in Lanarkshire. Bellside village consisted of Bellside Co-operative, Bellside Pub, Peggy Kerr's sweet shop and Dinger's sweet shop – two sweet shops with maybe only a population of 300 people to serve.

My childhood was quite simply the happiest time of my life and I would never swap anything for what I had at home. We may never have had any great wealth but the summers were long and adventurous and the winters cold and with so much snow we kept a shovel outside the back door of the cottage to dig ourselves out in the morning.

The cottage only had three rooms and a kitchen. The girls, Agnes, Jean and Lorna, all slept in one room and the five boys in another. Then there was my parents' room which was out of bounds – and they must have had plenty of peace in there to produce so many children. I slept top to tail with my brothers which was quite awkward for me because two of them were bed-wetters. I was swimming for Scotland by the time I was five! Just joking! But there were occasional accidents that we'd all blame each other for.

I can never remember being poor. Sometimes we had to turn the shirts outside in when they were dirty or turn the collars on shirts when they were frayed but we were better off than most as there were some really poor kids at school. Some would have to go to school during the winter – and these were severe winters – in gutties (plimsoles). We never really reached those depths. Our family always owned the house we lived in rather than rented a council one. So, although we were never rich, we were never desperately poor either.

Mayfield Cottage, where we lived and were all born, had been built by my grandfather who'd come over from Strabahn in Ireland, at the age of thirteen, as a stowaway on a ship. He was from a big family as well. I suppose they wouldn't even have missed him as it would have been one less mouth to feed. His name was Hugh Devine and, seemingly, he was a very clever man. He owned a petrol station in Bellside, on the main Airdrie to Carlisle road and my father inherited that when he died. It was really just four petrol pumps and a shack but it allowed my dad to quit the mines to man the pumps. That didn't make us particularly better off but everyone was happy, which was the most important thing.

The morning I was born, one of the petrol pumps had broken down and they had phoned for a fitter to come out and repair it, which he duly did. The fitter asked my father how my mother was because he knew she was expecting. My dad replied, 'It's funny you should ask because she had a

3

baby boy this morning.' The repairman congratulated him and was really made up because the 11th of January was his birthday too. Then he asked my dad what they were going to call me. My father liked the coincidence of the repairman and I sharing the same birthday so he named me on the spot after Sydney Borland, the petrol pump repairman – and that was that. Until the day he died, Sydney Borland sent me a birthday card every year and, even long after his death, Sydney's widow and his daughter kept up the tradition. You couldn't hope to meet a nicer person than Sydney Borland and I'm proud that he was the man I got my name from.

You always hear of the Protestant–Catholic divide but, while I was growing up in my little bit of Lanarkshire, I honestly don't remember it being a factor at all. Maybe there was more togetherness because of the war, I just don't know. I used to go to church and Sunday School and there were the usual separate Catholic and Protestant schools in Cleland but it was no big thing. Although I went to Cleland Public, the Protestant school, I played with the kids from the other school without thought or hesitation. There was no division in my world – some of my best friends were Catholic and the same was true for my mother and father.

I loved school. You had card swapping, conkers, bools and marbles, the girls had skipping ropes and we played football. It seemed like all the entertainment was free in those days too and, at night, all the family sat round the wireless, listening to *Dick Barton Special Agent*. There was also the Scottish Home Service, playing Scottish Country Dance music and featuring bands like those of Jimmy Shand, Jim Cameron and all the others of that era. Then, on a Sunday afternoon, it was Ronnie Ronald who was a whistler and that's how my fascination with entertainment started. I realised I could whistle from a very young age – I was probably ten or eleven – and I used to impersonate birds on my way to school. Even to this day, I can still do it – it's quite easy when you know how. During the mating season in early spring, I'm sure the blackbirds thought there was a potential mate in the area because, whenever I started whistling, they'd go crazy and start leaping around the branches. A local newspaper did an article on me, saying I was 'the boy who could charm the birds down from the trees'.

Then the *Sunday Mail* picked up on the story and, as a result of that, I was invited to the BBC in Glasgow's Queen Margaret Drive to meet a lady called Kathleen Garscadden. She was known as Auntie Kathleen and was the head of BBC Radio Scotland at that time. I was to take part in a Sunday broadcast with my idol Ronnie Ronald himself, the whistler who had inspired me. He used to do a song called 'If I Were a Blackbird' and I'd whistle along to it and just copy everything he was doing. I suppose it was a big deal at the time but I never thought of it in that way – nothing really fazed me as a child. Auntie Kathleen invited me to perform on the radio again when I was about twelve and, this time, I sang 'A Gordon for Me'. This song was associated with the Gordon Highlanders and had been recorded by Robert Wilson, a huge star at the time, and, unbeknown to me, it would become very prominent in the early years of my life.

By this time, I was also on the *Go As You Please* circuit, a touring talent show that was the 1950s equivalent of *Stars In Your Eyes* or *Opportunity Knocks*. You'd enter a competition and, if you won, you'd get paid – maybe a pound for the winner, ten bob for second and five bob for third. You could be performing anywhere in Lanarkshire – Larkhall, Carluke, Cleland, Wishaw. Of course, being so young – I was around twelve to thirteen at this time – I won umpteen of the contests. In the early 50s, a pound was a lot of money but most of the money I won would be spent on a new kilt, stage clothes, travelling expenses and things like that.

I suppose I became a bit of a celebrity but Cleland was a wonderful place where you could be brought down to earth very quickly. One of Cleland's most famous sons was Jim Delaney, a footballer of great distinction. With cup-winner's medals for Celtic, Manchester United and Derry City, to this day he is the only player to have won three cup-winner's medals in three countries – Scotland, England and Ireland. He also helped to beat England in 1935, when he scored in the King George V Jubilee match at Hampden. The result was 4–2 and the story goes that, on the evening after this famous victory, he was standing outside the pub door in Cleland, chatting to people, while having a fag and a pint, as if it was the most natural thing in the world. And, if anyone asked him about his goal, he'd just shrug and say, 'Och, I was just in the right place at the right time.'

Another famous footballer from Cleland was Joe Jordan. Joe's father, Frank, was the manager of local Co-operative. Joe was from a later era so I never really knew him but I do remember his father well. For such a wee place, it didn't half produce some great players.

I played football but not like these fellas. Like the rest of my family, it was more performing I was into. My sister Agnes played the piano, my brother Hugh wasn't too bad on the accordion and my father could play the moothie. More or less every Saturday night, there was music in the house.

My father sometimes went to the local inn for a couple of beers – it certainly wouldn't be much more than that in those days because it was very expensive. His favourite tipple was 'a half and a half', which was a half measure of whisky and a half pint of beer but most of the time he couldn't afford spirits and would just have beer. Invariably, his night at the pub would lead to a party back at our cottage and they'd ask the kids to do Al Jolson songs or some Sinatra, while I was whistling away. It was fantastic and an idyllic way to grow up – although social workers would probably label us deprived these days!

When I wasn't performing in the house on a Saturday night, I was doing local shows for the old age pensioners, called Old Folks' Treats, or performing at charity shows. There was a boy in Cleland called Jim O'Brien and I think he'd lost an eye through some kind of accident. Then someone threw a stone at him and he lost the other eye so he was totally blind. The priest wanted to send him to Lourdes to see if there was any miracle cure so I used to do a show for him, at the chapel hall in Cleland, to try to raise some money. As I said, religion didn't come into it – he was just a boy who needed some money and everyone tried to chip in and do their bit, regardless of what faith they were.

There were two pits near our cottage and one was called The Monkey – for reasons I never discovered – and there was a burn that we used to dam and swim in during the summer. It's funny how times change though because I once took my oldest son, Gary, up there years later and told him I'd show him what I used to do as a boy. It was a nice warm day and I got my swimming costume on and went down into the burn and started collecting bricks to dam it so we could swim but, halfway through, he asked me what the time was. I said we had plenty of time but he insisted *The Lone Ranger* would be coming on soon and he wanted to go home. He just wasn't interested but our folks used to have to drag my friends and me out of that dam for our tea. Different times, eh?

But the best bit about living so close to the pits was that the miners had to pass our front gate. We'd be outside begging for their pieces (the sandwiches they took to work with them) and the guys would say, 'I'll get you on the way back, son.' There was something magical about a miner's piece. The piece boxes in those days were made of aluminium and they looked like an old-fashioned biscuit tin, rounded at the top then square down the sides – exactly the same size and shape as a loaf. A miner's piece was butter, jam and cheese between two slices of bread. I still make my oldest grandson Ryan a miner's piece as he's always loved them. If you were lucky, when the miners were coming back from the pits after a shift, they might have a piece left over and, if they did and they gave it to you, it felt like you'd won the lottery. To this day, the memory of them makes my mouth water.

When I was thirteen, I spent the summer holidays working for a farmer called Sandy Bankier. Sandy's farm was near Cleland and I would do things like mucking out the cowsheds and bringing in the hay. I remember I once said to him, 'There's nothing to do.' This is about the worst thing you can say to a farmer. He went and got a drum of green paint and a wire brush and had me scrape all the old paint off all the barn doors then paint them with this thick green paint. It was back-breaking work and, even now, I refuse to have anything painted green anywhere, even in the garden – I can't stand the memories it brings back. I saw Sandy in 2004 at a school fête I opened in Cleland. He wasn't very well but we were both delighted to see each other again – and, diplomatically, neither of us brought up the subject of the green paint!

After that first summer, Sandy asked if I'd be willing to work weekends for him and I gladly agreed. Another time when there wasn't much to do, he dropped me off in one of his fields. It was about fifteen to twenty acres in size and all that was in it was piles of dung scattered everywhere. Sandy handed me a fork and told me to spread the dung all over the field. Nowadays, they have dung spreaders for this but, back then, it was all done by hand. However, I did it and I've still got the calluses on my hands to prove it. Can you imagine the response you'd get if you asked a thirteen-year-old to do that now?

I worked on Sandy's farm every summer for three years, doing everything from driving the tractor, making the silage, bringing in the coos to mucking out the cowsheds. One day, one of the tractor lads jumped me while I was coming out the shed with a bale of hay on my back. I got such a fright that I dropped the bale and it fell on my heel and broke my ankle. I walked home that night just thinking it was sore, and went to work for the next two days before realising that a bone in my ankle had actually snapped. The work and the play may have been hard but I'd recommend to anybody to do six months on a Scottish farm because the breakfast and the lunches you get are the best you'll ever experience in your life – anywhere in the world.

I was quite well paid too and, because I was what they called casual labour, I got better wages than the boys working on the farm full-time – maybe that's why they were always winding me up! But the pay was nothing compared to what I could earn doing a gig.

Every village has its characters and none more so than Cleland. One was a man who, for reasons best known to himself, was called Cocky Rodgers. Then there was Alice Sweeney. She was a lovely lady but she had a bald head and always wore a tammy. Another was Picky Haddy, who got his name because he was always picking his nose. Breechy Dillett was so-called because his shorts were too long.

And then there was Tommy Owens, a hunchback. One night, Tommy was coming back to Cleland on the last bus from Wishaw and he was the only person on the bus. It was a pretty rickety old bus and, rather than have it actually stop at Cleland to let Tommy off, the driver told the bus conductor to tell Tommy he would just slow down enough for him to jump off at Cleland Cross. So, as they approached Tommy's stop and the bus began to slow down, the conductor shouted, 'Jump, Tommy!' But the bus was going just a bit too fast so Tommy turned to the conductor and said, 'This is a hump I've got on my back – no' a f***ing parachute!'

It was the days of the Teddy boys and Tommy, God rest his soul, always wanted to dress in the latest fashions so he had the velvet collar, the blue suede shoes and the long jacket. Some may think, with a disfigurement like Tommy's, he wouldn't want to draw attention to himself – not oor Tommy.

For entertainment, there was always the snooker hall in the Cleland Welfare which was opposite my school. We used to nip in there at night to have a few frames. We had a good snooker team in Cleland and sometimes they would go and play at places like St Francis in Glasgow and I'd be taken along to do a wee bit of entertainment after the competition was over.

Back in the 50s, the pubs closed at 9.30 p.m. so, most Saturday nights after chucking out time, the men would go and kindle a bonfire on some waste ground and throw potatoes on the fire. Then, at some point, someone would produce an accordion and there'd be a real old sing-song. It was absolutely magic and a grin still spreads across my face when I think of those days – especially one night in particular. Bunny Anderson, a local man, was a huge fella who could eat fish suppers like they were going out of fashion. Well, he had nipped behind a bush to relieve himself during one of these shindigs and, just as he was sitting back down, my pal and I put a couple of penny bangers under his backside and we just about blew his arse off! He was well sloshed by this time and he had no idea what was going on but the whole place ended up roaring with laughter. However, the real bonus of these party nights was that, on the following Monday, I would take the empty beer bottles back and, as you got a penny or tuppence per beer bottle, I'd make a small fortune.

And it wasn't just me and my pals who were having fun – everyone always seemed to be enjoying themselves. I'm sure youngsters are sick of hearing this but it really was the sort of community where you never had to lock your doors at night – never.

The local men also used to run massive tossing schools in which they gambled illegally on the outcome of tossed coins. It was a men-only affair and sometimes youngsters, like myself, were brought along to look out for the police. There could be a congregation of anything from 100 to 200 men. It was a game of two pennies and the players would place them on their fingers and flip them up in the air. The rest then bet on the result of the two coins coming down. Heads paid out, tails you lost. But, if it was one heads and one tails, you did it again until you a got a winner. But the stakes soon mounted up and sometimes you had as much as £200 to £300 on the toss of two coins. It was big, big money in those days.

The big tossing schools were held in Wishaw and New-mains but every village had its own in secret places, at the back of some hills or wherever – places where you could see the police coming from a fair distance. They very seldom got busted as the police tended to turn a blind eye. Can you imagine them having to arrest all those men and write down all their names? This was in the days before the police were swamped with paperwork and they hated writing. So, in all the years I was a lookout for the tossing schools, I never heard of anybody actually being caught.

I used to love the whole experience – from being asked to take part by the men of the village and then hearing the cries of excitement or the roars of disappointment. It was all part of the community and it built an incredible spirit. Put it this way, you couldn't imagine 200 men gathering these days to play a game with two pennies and have a laugh along the way. But that's what I loved about Bellside and I can remember those tossing schools as if they were only yesterday.

When I was a kid, one of my best pals was a boy called Sandy Nicol who ended up working for one of the big companies out in Hong Kong. Sadly, I attended his funeral in 2003. He had a heart attack and died. But I used to play with Sandy and his brother Jimmy Nicol, who I still bump into occasionally. Then there was Ian Watson, Alex Allan and, of course, Bobby Young, who was the best man at my wedding. Sadly, I attended Bobby's funeral in 2005 but I still bump into the rest of them as I make sure I go back to Cleland once a year, just to have a look around and remember my glorious childhood. It can sometimes be embarrassing when I meet old school pals and I don't remember them. At that school fête I attended, there were people who'd been in my class and, frankly, I got the shock of my life as I hadn't seen them for maybe forty years. It wasn't that they had aged badly, it's just that you always have this picture in your mind of how they

---

back of some hills or wherever – places where you could see the police coming from a fair distance. They very seldom got busted as the police tended to turn a blind eye. Can you imagine them having to arrest all those men and write down all their names? This was in the days before the police were swamped with paperwork and they hated writing. So, in all the years I was a lookout for the tossing schools, I never heard of anybody actually being caught.

I used to love the whole experience – from being asked to take part by the men of the village and then hearing the cries of excitement or the roars of disappointment. It was all part of the community and it built an incredible spirit. Put it this way, you couldn't imagine 200 men gathering these days to play a game with two pennies and have a laugh along the way. But that's what I loved about Bellside and I can remember those tossing schools as if they were only yesterday.

When I was a kid, one of my best pals was a boy called Sandy Nicol who ended up working for one of the big companies out in Hong Kong. Sadly, I attended his funeral in 2003. He had a heart attack and died. But I used to play with Sandy and his brother Jimmy Nicol, who I still bump into occasionally. Then there was Ian Watson, Alex Allan and, of course, Bobby Young, who was the best man at my wedding. Sadly, I attended Bobby's funeral in 2005 but I still bump into the rest of them as I make sure I go back to Cleland once a year, just to have a look around and remember my glorious childhood. It can sometimes be embarrassing when I meet old school pals and I don't remember them. At that school fête I attended, there were people who'd been in my class and, frankly, I got the shock of my life as I hadn't seen them for maybe forty years. It wasn't that they had aged badly, it's just that you always have this picture in your mind of how they used to look and suddenly you're confronted by this person you don't recognise. They said it wasn't as bad for them as they'd seen me on a regular basis in newspapers or on the telly but I didn't have that advantage and it really was a shock to my system.

But that doesn't really matter. What is important is that my whole childhood was spent being part of a great family and a fantastic community.

2

I'M A TV SENSATION!

By around the early 1950s, television was just starting to grip the nation and Auntie Kathleen from the BBC invited me to appear on a television show called *All Your Own*. It was one of those programmes where they got contestants from Scotland, England, Ireland and Wales to represent their country doing all sorts of things. Some people did Highland dancing, others Irish dancing, while one fella was on just because he could make toy soldiers out of toothpaste tubes, as in those days the tubes were made out of zinc. It was presented by Cliff Michelmore, who was mega famous, and Hugh Weldon, who went on to become Sir Hugh Weldon, Director General of the BBC. The piano player was a fellow called Steve Race, one of the finest jazz musicians to ever come out of London. So Auntie Kathleen put my name forward to represent Scotland and it was arranged for me to go down to the BBC studios in London's Shepherds Bush.

There was no pre-recording in those days and the show would be going out live. Not only would it be my first time on television but my first time out of Scotland. I remember there was hell to pay though because I had to get permission to take one day off school and they wouldn't let me. That was down to the headmaster Mr Murray – a right old b*****d – who was putting the blocks on it. I was attending Cleland Junior Secondary School by then and I can't remember if he finally relented because of pressure from my mum or the BBC or a bit of both but I was finally allowed to travel to London on the Friday for the live Saturday show. As you can imagine it was quite a big deal for a thirteen-year-old to be going off to do a television show in London but no one from the school was allowed to come to the station to see me off. The irony is that the local parish priest and the headmaster from the Catholic school turned up at the station to wish me luck but that old bugger Murray did nothing. What a petty man.

So I set off from Cleland to Glasgow, then Glasgow to London with my mum and a suitcase for my kilts. I can remember the smell of Glasgow Central to this day – the steam, the coal and the grease all creating that unique atmosphere of an old-fashioned station. But my mother and I went hungry all the way to London as we hadn't had the sense to get a sandwich – well, we were hardly seasoned travellers. On arriving in London, we had to take a taxi to the hotel, which had all been arranged by the BBC. I don't remember much of the hotel or the taxi journey but I do remember how it felt stepping into the television studio for the first time. Everything was taken very, very seriously and it was drummed into us that, if you made a mistake, there was no way to rectify it and the whole nation would basically see you make an arse of yourself – although they didn't quite put it in those terms.

But fortunately children just don't have fear and I went on and sang 'A Gordon for Me' and whistled a tune called 'Tritsch-Tratsch Polka' by Strauss flawlessly, without a hint of nerves, as if I was performing on a Saturday night in our cottage back home. Everything seemed to pass in a blur and, before I knew it, I had been beamed live across the entire country. Afterwards, everyone spoke to me – even the host Cliff Michelmore. Steve Race gave me a card that said 'To a

proper trooper' and Hugh Weldon penned 'To a real pro' –
not bad for someone at the age of thirteen.

Then it was off to catch the train home sharpish. I did the
show at around 5 o'clock and we had to be back at the station
for 8 o'clock to board the sleeper. Although I remember
nothing about my first-ever taxi ride when I arrived in the
capital, I certainly remember the return journey from the
BBC as the driver asked, 'Aren't you the lad who was just
on the TV?' It really shows you the power television – just a
few hours after I'd appeared and even the taxi driver knew
me – and that was when TV was in its infancy.

I actually never saw the show myself so I've no idea how
I did on it but everyone else seemed to think it went well.
There was only one television in the whole of Bellside. It was
in Peggy Kerr's sweet shop so the entire population of this
little mining village flocked to Peggy's shop to try to see me.
I went back to school on the Monday morning and, if people
thought of me any differently after my fifteen minutes of
fame, I certainly didn't notice.

But, after London, things would never be quite the same
for me again. I had probably decided before I went there that
I was destined for a life onstage. I had no interest in school
any more and the way that the headmaster, Mr Murray, had
tried to block my television debut probably compounded
that feeling. So the stage was set and, after I'd had a taste for
it, I wanted more.

While the reaction from fellow pupils had been one of
indifference, the papers were all over me and, more impor-
tantly, Robert Wilson had watched the show. As I've said,
Robert Wilson was, in Scotland anyway, a big star. He was a
legendary entertainer. Everyone knew him and he was simply
called 'The Voice of Scotland'. Robert sent me a letter saying

he had watched me perform his song 'A Gordon for Me' and he would like to meet me. This was big news because, apart from being so famous, Robert was also something of a local hero as he was born and bred in a place called Newarthill which is about two and a half miles from Cleland. My folks couldn't believe it. This was serious stuff and suddenly we found ourselves in a different league. He came to the house and Mum, Dad and all my brothers and sisters waited eagerly to meet him. I remember him pulling up outside in a fabulous car. It was an Austin Sheerline and it looked like a Rolls Royce – we'd never seen anything like it. Our cottage was up the hill in the village so we were kind of isolated but here was this huge star with his big flashy car sitting outside our wee place.

After all the introductions, he arranged to teach me. I remember how handsome he was. He had the true look of a star and he was a big, big man who filled the doorway. He spoke to my parents and told them how very impressed he'd been by my performance. He said he would like to give me voice coaching as he wanted me to release a record. Once he'd found the right song for me, I would rehearse with him and he'd show me how to sing it. Shortly afterwards, he sent tickets for me and my mother to watch him at the Alhambra Theatre in Glasgow. His signature tune was 'Down in the Glen' and he'd perform it onstage in full Crawford highland dress – socks and a white doublet with a jabot and a piper's plaid over his shoulder. He looked immaculate – absolutely phenomenal. The place was packed but we had the best seats in the house and, of course, we got to meet him backstage afterwards – he really had gone to town for us. After that night, I said, 'This is it – this is where I want to be.' And I just couldn't wait to leave school.

The following week, Robert got back in contact because he'd found a couple of songs he thought would be suitable. One was called 'Betty Fitchett's Wedding' and the one for the other side was 'Lunan Bay', which celebrates a beauty spot just south of Montrose. 'Betty Fitchett's Wedding' was written by Jimmy Shand. They were to be recorded on the first take. And so, at Langside Halls in Glasgow's South Side, with a choir called the Scottish Junior Singers conducted by Agnes Duncan, I cut my first record. Before we did the recording, Agnes was getting the choir to practise their singing using that old favourite 'Auld Lang Syne' and, apparently, there was a bit of a stooshie because one of the kids was singing 'auld *Langside*' instead of 'auld lang syne'!

The record was eventually released but it didn't do spectacularly well. And, as for money, well, I can't remember ever receiving anything. I think it was played on the radio but, bear in mind, there were very few stations in those days – there was the BBC and that was it. If a record didn't get played on the BBC, it just didn't get played. Shortly after I recorded that first record, Robert was doing a song called 'Cottage by the Lea'. It's an Irish song and part of the chorus goes:

> From down a lane that winds behind the garden,
> The blackbird greets the smiling summer morn.

As soon as I heard him mention the word 'blackbird', I had to do a birdcall. And it got me on to Robert's next recording.

I flew from Glasgow Airport down to London on a turbo-prop plane and arrived at HMV which would eventually become the famous Abbey Road Studios. As ever, my mother came with me and it was our first time on a flight. It was just unbelievable for us – absolutely mind-blowing. I remember, as the plane was heading up into the sky, I was reading an article in *The People* which Robert had written and he actually mentioned me in it – so I was on a plane and in the paper at the same time. Robert had written, 'I've done many things in my life but I've never had to pay money to fly a young man all the way from Glasgow to London to give me the bird!' I never discovered if that song was a hit or not – I honestly didn't care. All I knew was I had got to go on a plane for the first time so nothing else really mattered.

After all that excitement, I landed myself an agent – of sorts. He was a blind man and his name was Stopher Morrison. Well, that was his nickname – his real name was Chris. He had offices in West Nile Street in Glasgow and my brother Hugh had a café right across from Stopher's offices.

It was great to have Hugh as a big brother. When I was about ten, he got me the best present I've ever had – a Hopalong Cassidy suit straight from America, complete with the chaps, shirt and everything – if only he'd known then what he was starting!

Because Hugh's café was also next door to the Glasgow Empire, he used to have a lot of showbiz stars coming in, including a young Jim Dale who later went on to be a star of the *Carry On* films. Jim was a Carroll Levis discovery. Carroll Levis hosted an *Opportunity Knocks* type of show during the 50s and 60s. It was a big, big show and Jim was one of its winners – probably the most famous one. Jim was a comic and he and other winners from the Carroll Levis talent shows would tour Scotland, putting on variety shows under the name of The Carroll Levis Discoveries. They were appearing at The Empire but, despite his rising profile, Jim was skint and, one Tuesday, he tapped my brother for ten bob, saying he would pay him back when he got his wages on the Friday. Every night, Hugh would give him tea or coffee for nothing because he never had any money – such was the harsh reality of these shows. The impresarios and agents like Levis always wanted the earth from their performers but then paid them next to nothing. This has been going on since time immemorial – they latch on to people who want to perform on the stage, promise them great deals and then take advantage of them by paying them workhouse fees.

My brother put up posters for the shows at The Empire and, in return for this form of advertising, he got two free tickets every week for Monday nights. So I saw everybody – Ronnie Ronald, Larry Parks, who played in the *Jolson Story*, and Mel Torme. I even saw Des O'Connor although, sadly, it was not on the night of the famous incident when he was dying onstage and pretended to faint to escape the notoriously difficult crowd.

I also got to meet Roy Rodgers, my hero as a young boy, and even his famous horse Trigger. But I think it was Ronnie Ronald, the famous whistler, who sticks out the most for me because, quite simply, I wanted to be him and the papers had already branded me Scotland's pocket-sized Ronnie Ronald. I'd mingle with most of the stars backstage and Ronnie, who I had met previously at the BBC, again just told me to stick at what I was doing.

Anyway, Stopher used to come into Hugh's café every day for a cup of coffee and he would get chatting to my brother who had obviously told him about me. On a Sunday evening, Stopher used to hire a bus and take people like Billy Dennison and ventriloquist Ken Swan up to the Caird Hall in Dundee to do shows there. Well, when I joined them, I'd never seen a bus like this in my life. It wasn't quite a double-decker, it was more like a deck and a half and I loved exploring it.

For my first show in Dundee, I remember copying Ronnie Ronald and whistling his signature tune 'Sweet Sixteen'. Then I'd do 'In A Monastery Garden', complete with birdcalls, and finish with 'A Gordon for Me'. That was it. The Caird Hall was absolutely mobbed and the place went crazy. I'm talking about there being an audience of 1,800 to maybe more than 2,000 – and that was on a Sunday night. After the show finished, the make-up came off quickly and it was back on to the bus for the journey home. But, before we left, Stopher would call each person individually to the back of the bus to pay them. When it came to my turn, he called my name out and said, 'Sydney, that's for you.' He handed me two packets of Wrigley's spearmint chewing gum – that was my wages for travelling up from Cleland to Glasgow, Glasgow to Dundee, killing them onstage and then going back home again. But I was actually quite happy with my lot because you couldn't get chewing gum then as sweets were still retained. Money just never came into my head.

It was only latterly that I considered money being part of the entertainment business. If everybody in entertainment was in it for the money, there'd be nobody in the business at all.

After Stopher's Dundee shows, I joined Annie Muir's Concert Party in Carluke. I first meet Annie when I had entered one of these *Go As You Please* contests. Annie was to play the piano so I gave her my music and whistled and sang 'Sweet Sixteen', 'Mockingbird' and 'A Gordon for Me'. That night, I won something like £3 which was a lot of money in those days. Also working the same circuit were Tom and Jack, the Alexander Brothers. I came across them occasionally doing these gigs and they lived only about five miles from me. They'd come into my father's petrol station on the main road and fill up before going to Airdrie or Perth or wherever so I knew them from a very, very young age. But, when I won the competition in Carluke, Annie Muir – although she was always Mrs Muir to me – asked if I'd be willing to come and join her and her 'renowned' Concert Party. Well, I jumped at the chance as The Annie Muir Concert Party was certainly renowned as she so eloquently put it.

We played lots of Old Folks' Treats where we'd put on a show for the auld yins. The shows consisted of Mrs Muir, who was a wonderful vocalist and a good piano player – not great but good. She used to teach me new songs and we'd rehearse maybe two nights a week. Also, in those days, there were no microphones so you just stood up and sang with the piano player. I remember one time somebody actually produced a microphone and no one knew how to use it. But Mrs Muir did a song called 'The Sunshine of Your Smile', which was a real tear jerker and a very hard act to follow.

Then there was John McMahon who was a baritone from Carluke. He had an absolutely incredible voice and his big number was 'Scotland Yet'. The last line of each verse was 'I'll drink a cup to Scotland yet' and it would just kill the audience every time. On top of that, he was great company. John should have been a star – and I'm talking a huge star – but I think he married a German girl who hated him going out at night even though he was probably making more over a weekend in these concerts than he actually did when working at his regular weekday job. He had the most incredible baritone voice I've ever heard in all my life and I have heard a lot of singers over the years.

Another favourite was Johnny Forrest, an accordionist and singer supreme who was also from Carluke – the pool of talent from there was quite incredible. Johnny was maybe three years older than me and we used to pal about together. He now lives in Vancouver, Canada, as does my brother Andy, and I still see Johnny almost every year. In fact, Johnny and I have been corresponding for the best part of fifty years. But, back then, he would perform some really popular songs on the accordion and he could sing a bit as well. He continued performing even when he moved to Canada and worked on *The Don Messer Show*, a huge TV programme that was probably the equivalent of Scotland's *The White Heather Club*. Johnny sold hundreds and thousands of records in Canada and is now a travel agent – well, I suppose he had to change careers when a family came along. Put it this way, one phrase you'll never hear is 'There goes the accordionist's Ferrari.'

Eleanor Thornton was part of the troupe too and not only was she a soprano she was also an absolute stunner – a real six-foot beauty and they were few and far between in Lanarkshire, believe me. Johnny and I would have given anything to have a wee canoodle with her! But we didn't stand a chance – Eleanor was well out of our league. And, to complete the party, there were Dave and Babs Irvine, from Motherwell, a comedian and his wife. They were both very, very funny. Dave, in particular, could have really made it big in showbiz but comedy was just a hobby to him. He worked in the steelworks or something and I thought that, if any of us was going to make it, it would have been Dave. I haven't been in touch with Dave since those days but, throughout the years, I always hoped that he would have given showbiz a go and that maybe I'd bump into him. I really thought this guy could have been as big as Chic Murray or Billy Connolly. Then there was Jack Jackley who was, would you believe, a country singer with a guitar!

Just occasionally Anne Muir – Mrs Muir's daughter – would join us as a tap dancer and singer. Whenever they needed an extra, they brought Anne in. She was a beautiful girl and, lo and behold, it turned out she really fancied me. But, unfortunately, at that time, I had my beady little eye on her pal, a girl called Lorna Yule. I saw Anne years later and I can honestly say I have few regrets but Anne was definitely one of them – she was still stunning. She had married a surgeon and was a professional in the medical field herself. I couldn't help thinking that maybe I should have paid more attention to Johnny when he told me that Anne was madly in love with me!

So this unique collection of talent – including me – would perform around most of the Lanarkshire area, from Coldburn to Carluke, Wishaw to Motherwell and Airdrie to Uddingston. It was a massive area and I don't think there was a social club, old folks' home, pigeon fanciers' club or gun club we didn't play. If these organisations held a dinner dance, invariably we were there doing our stuff.

I was paid decent wages of ten bob a gig but I seldom saw a penny of it as there were always members of the family who needed it more than I did. One week my sister would need money to pay her electricity bill, the next week it would be something else. All my life, money has never mattered. I know it's easy to say that when you've got a few quid but it was never ever, even to this day, a driving factor for me. All I ever wanted to do, from the days of Annie Muir and her wonderful Concert Party, was to perform.

Sometimes the venues were so far away, in places like Leven, that we had to hire transport from a local woman called Bessie Allan. Bessie had a wee baker's van and we used to borrow it and my brother-in-law Jackie Prentice drove it. But there was no heating in this van and, in the depths of winter – when winters really were winters – we each used to take hot water bottles and clutch on to them for the entire journey, in a vain attempt to try to keep warm. I'd perform at a *Go As You Please* competition and then I'd make sure I filled up the bottle with hot water for the way back. It was absolutely freezing and it felt like some of those journeys were never going to end. Sometimes I'd have to use my prize money to fill the van up with petrol. If I was placed in a competition, the prize money would just about cover the cost of the petrol. If I won, there might be a little left over so that was extra incentive to do as well as I could!

When I started working with Annie, I began to do fewer and fewer of these competitions. I remember we put on some incredible shows for some wee working men's social clubs. One time, we were playing the town hall in Carluke for some celebration or another. The band that was on before us was Jim Freeman's and he and his troupe came from Motherwell. Jim didn't have any hair so he used to put black boot polish on his head instead – sheer madness but the crowd didn't care, they loved him.

I must have worked with Annie for about two years and, during this time, I performed nearly every weekend. I was actually making not bad money – ten bob a night was good going for someone in their early teens. It was even possible I was earning more than my dad but there was never any resentment directed towards me and, as I said, I certainly never saw any of the money anyway because we had a big family and my mother always found a good home for whatever I earned.

There were some other great characters around at that time too. There was a woman who dressed up as a man. Her stage name was Master Joe Peterson and her most famous song was 'Choir Boy' – she sounded just like a boy soprano and was an absolutely phenomenal singer. Then there were The Mansfield Singers, a bunch of close-harmony singers who were headed up by a fella called Jock Garden from Kilsyth, and I'd perform about half a dozen shows a year with them in various places, from the Isle of Arran up to Inverness. Jock Garden was the uncle of my musical director of over thirty years' standing, Bill Garden. Bill's grandfather's claim to fame was that he was the man who invented the scrolling blackboard.

Performing really was my lifeblood and, with all these shows all around the country, I was now absolutely desperate to leave school. I eventually walked out the school gates at the age of fifteen, without a single qualification to my name. I feel now that I should have paid more attention to my school work because I wasn't stupid but I simply had no notion for it. There was plenty of work available and I could have easily have been a motor mechanic, a plumber, a joiner or anything like that as there were so many apprenticeships in trades on offer. But I didn't fancy any of them. I remember when I left school I applied for a job in a tailor's shop in Wishaw. Two days before I was supposed to start, I got word to say I'd passed the audition to be the juvenile lead in *Wild Grows the Heather*, in London. This was a musical based on J. M. Barrie's *The Little Minister* and it was to be staged at the Hippodrome in Leicester Square, which is now Stringfellows.

That marked the start of my professional life in show business – *and*, before it had even started, the abrupt end of my career in menswear!

3

THE BIG SMOKE

I had gone along for the musical's auditions in Glasgow. I'd heard about it as there had been a lot of publicity in the papers. The reports were all saying that one lucky boy could land the lead in this brand new musical called *Wild Grows the Heather* in London's West End and that lucky boy turned out to be yours truly.

The auditions were for the part of Micah Dow, the mole catcher's son, and they were held at the Alhambra Theatre in Waterloo Street, Glasgow. I took to the stage wearing a kilt and I whistled 'Tristch-Trastch Polka', which had become my party piece, and then I sang 'A Gordon for Me' and 'Mockingbird'. I performed in front of a guy called Ralph Reader, who was the producer of the *Gang Shows*, and the famous London theatre impresario Jack Waller, who was funding the whole project. He backed a lot of shows in the West End at that time, including musicals like *Call Me Madam*. After that, I heard nothing until, one day, out of the blue, a letter arrived. I couldn't believe what it said:

> Dear Sydney,
> You've had a very successful audition . . .
> Sign your contract and return it . . .
> You'll need a London agent . . .

It was like a dream. Basically, that letter was my ticket into showbiz.

The next thing I knew I was in all the papers. It was a big deal. In fact, it would still be a big deal today, I suppose, if a young boy from Cleland landed the juvenile lead in a West End musical. In football terms, it would be the equivalent of being picked to play striker for Scotland. As for my family, it simply meant that, while I was away, my mother would be away too as I had be chaperoned. Fortunately for my family's sake – but unfortunately for my fledgling career – we wouldn't be away that long. I think, in total, the musical ran for about twenty weeks. It was supposed to last twenty years as all the talk was that it was going to run and run and be as big in the West End as *The Mousetrap*. It was a Scottish musical but, as it turned out, it was too Scottish for London's tastes and the critics reckoned it was all just too parochial.

However, for the twenty weeks that it did run, I was in heaven. I was making about £28 a week – phenomenal wages for a fifteen year old in 1955 and I probably made more in a week than my dear old dad made in a month. Not that I got to strut around the place like the big 'I am' – no, no. As usual, I never saw any of the money – my mum looked after all that!

Although the critics mauled the show, surprisingly I managed to escape their criticism. I remember one report said that I was one of 'the *Heather*'s purple patches', while another added that 'the boy whistler was the highlight of the show'. So I came out of the disaster fairly well. I wouldn't say I was devastated by the show being slated as I didn't really think about it because I was just too busy. Every night, you had this stuff called bowl to put on your arms, legs, face and what have you. It was basically just fake tan – which is all the rage these days – because the setting was supposed to be summertime in Scotland. Obviously the person who decided that it would be necessary, for the sake of authenticity, to have the cast looking suntanned had never been to Scotland in the summertime.

We actually opened at the Palace Theatre in Manchester and then did a stint at The Empire in Edinburgh. All the new shows were taken on a tour of the country in order to get everything sorted out before they were unleashed on the discerning West End. To avoid the pasting our show got, maybe we should have taken it on a longer tour!

Our musical director was Lewis Stone, a little Jewish guy who, in those days, was as big as Glenn Miller. Lewis Stone had his own orchestra and he was truly a phenomenal musician. For me, going from Annie Muir's 'renowned' Concert Party to suddenly appearing in big theatres and working alongside legends like Stone was a big step up. The one thing I quickly learned was that you had to be a lot more disciplined. You went through the same thing every night and it had to be exactly the same because other people on the stage depended on you. Before, I had had the leeway just to do my own thing and improvise but now there were actors who were waiting for their cues. Actors are actors and they want everything to be precise so I had to be a lot more disciplined in that respect. Many, many years later, when I was in panto at the Gaiety in Ayr with Gwyneth Guthrie from *Take the High Road*, I remember something happened in the audience one night and I spent about ten minutes just improvising. Meanwhile, poor Gwyneth was still standing there all the time, patiently waiting for me to deliver a line she could respond to. I eventually said, 'Don't worry, I'll come back to you – I haven't forgotten your line.' Actors – they can't do anything until you give them their cue. Back then though, I was the boy and was certainly treated as one.

But then, just to make matters worse, I was only about five or six weeks into the show when my voice broke so I went from a really high voice to great, big deep voice. Just like Aled Jones's voice, mine broke right in the middle of a song. At first, I didn't know what had happened and the audience began laughing. I couldn't work it out and I just kept thinking, 'What the hell is going on here?' This being showbiz though, I just had to get through it and, luckily enough, I only had one song left to perform. After that show, we had a consultation about it and decided that we'd rearrange the songs a bit so I could sing them lower and it worked out fine.

The leading girl in the musical was Eira Heath, a Welsh lass, but I never had the hots for her as she was about twenty-three at the time. No, the object of my desire was even older than Eira – and she was married. But, despite these obvious obstacles, she would be responsible for turning the boy Sydney into a man.

4

MY WOMEN

My first schoolboy crush was a fancy wee dame called Jean Montgomery. I saw her quite recently and she's wearing very well. But, when I was thirteen, she was a real looker and I used to fancy her like crazy at school. However, I don't think the feeling was mutual as we never went out or even kissed but she was definitely the first girl to catch my eye. The first girl I got to kiss was Mary McCormick. When I was about fourteen, we used to go to Green's Playhouse in Wishaw. This was one of five picture houses in Wishaw but today the town doesn't have a single cinema left. Mary and I often went to Green's on a Saturday night. It was the most popular picture house for boys of fourteen as, unlike other picture houses, the lights in Green's never came up. Even during the interval they kept it dark and, for that reason alone, they did a lot of business. And I'm certain I'm not the only one who doesn't remember any of the movies they were showing. There was plenty of hanky-panky going on in Green's Playhouse. What we got up to probably wouldn't surprise the kids nowadays but it would certainly have shocked our families to know what was going on back then.

A lot of teenagers lost their innocence in that place. I didn't go that far with Mary during the three months we lasted. We'd maybe have a wee kiss and, if I was lucky, I might have got the occasional brush against her breasts – completely accidental, of course. In those days, girls and women wore nylons held up by suspender belts and the boys all called that area of bare skin between the top of the stockings and the line of the pants 'the comedy zone' because, if you got as far as that, you were laughing. Sadly, although I'm sure she had one, I never got anywhere near Mary's 'comedy zone'. Mary was a brunette and, funnily enough, in my younger years, most of the girls I fancied had dark hair. There was one blonde-ish girl called Isobel McConnell and she was someone else from my school days that I met at the Cleland school fête in 2004.

After Isobel, there was a girl called Agnes Black and I had been seeing her for nearly two years, when my mum scared her off! One day, Agnes tried to come and see me while I was working on the farm but my eagle-eyed mother spotted her and chased her up the road shouting, 'You leave my son alone!' Not much got past Old Nellie, that's for sure.

I didn't have much money for all this dating as I hadn't started working so I used to go round all my sisters on a Saturday morning and scrounge some money from each of them. Then I had enough to take my girlfriend to the cinema and buy a packet of fags – yes, I was a teeny smoker, like everyone else seemed to be back then.

But, as lovely as they all were, I couldn't really call any of these young ladies my first real girlfriend. Now I have never told anyone this before, not even my wife Shirley (so when you're reading this, dear, try not to spill the tea). But, at the tender age of sixteen, I fancied a woman twice my age. She was the production assistant on the show and, because I would never disrespect a woman's honour or kiss and tell, let's just say her name was Kathleen – to protect the not-so-innocent. Well, Kathleen's job was to make sure the props were all in their right place. I couldn't help noticing that this gorgeous woman had started paying more and more attention to me. At first, I thought it was my imagination. I mean, why would this absolutely beautiful lady, with her long, reddish-auburn hair, be interested in a wee boy from Bellside? But, as it turned out, she was.

Of course, before anything could happen, we had the problem of my chaperone – Old Nellie. Fortunately, after a while, Mum started coming to the theatre at night less and less and that meant I could start seeing more and more of Kathleen. She definitely stirred an awakening in parts that hadn't been stirred like that before and, once I had put my hand in the sweetie jar, I wanted to keep coming back. How we didn't get caught I'll never know as we were at it as often as possible. The first time we did it was in my dressing room at The Empire in Edinburgh. I knew something was going to happen as earlier she had made her intentions perfectly clear. It was all quite nerve-racking, to say the least. The first one was a waste of time as I must have lasted all of about five seconds. But, when you're young, it doesn't take long to stoke the fire again so we had a repeat performance about ten minutes later.

After that, I think we must have done it every night. It was always before going on stage and there was no hanky panky in between performances as, even though I was very young, I always tried to be as professional about my work as possible. Any bonuses like Kathleen had to be put in their proper place.

We also had to make sure we were as discrete as possible as Kathleen was married – it really was a dangerous liaison. You may think that, at my age, the attention of this married woman would have blown my mind and I would have fallen head over heels in love with her. But the truth is that all I kept thinking was 'I hope my mother doesn't find out'. Our affair became all the more difficult when we went back to London because it seemed like Mum was always about. There was the added problem that Kathleen lived in London so, of course, she was staying with her husband again. She returned to her own life and slipped out of my grasp. So London was not only the death knell for *Wild Grows the Heather*, it was also the final curtain on my lusty affair with the beautiful Kathleen – or so I thought.

I never saw her much during our show's short run in the West End. We did attend the same cast parties and such like but she was always there with her husband. I found this embarrassing in itself and seeing them together made me feel very, very uncomfortable – and not just because of what he might do to me if he found out I had been sleeping with his gorgeous wife. It was a strange time all round. I was in the awkward situation of being able to see Kathleen but not being able to touch her and the way she went back to her old life so easily made me squirm.

Meanwhile, a dark cloud was hanging over the whole future of the show. The funny thing is that, by the time we had reached London, we thought we had a fantastic production. We had really tightened it up and felt we could take on the world but the theatre critics had other ideas. It just shows you how hard it is to be impartial when you see it from the cast's point of view. So, in amongst all these mixed emotions over Kathleen, I also had the disillusionment of the show not doing well to contend with too.

But the poor reviews didn't seem to put a damper on the non-stop socialising that went on. I remember one night our producer, Ralph Reader, threw a huge party at his plush Belgravia apartment, which was simply out of this world. I attended with Mum of course – my almost ever-present chaperone – and the first thing that struck me about his place was that all the photographs were of handsome young boys. The waiters serving drinks and food were all handsome young boys too. Reader started chatting to my mother and I overheard him saying, 'Mrs Devine, anytime you want to go home to Scotland to see the rest of your family, don't worry about Sydney – I'll take good care of him.' Well, he may have thought my mum was just some wee ordinary wifie from Scotland but the first thing Old Nellie said to me when we talked about it was 'No bloody way!' She had spent most of her days in Bellside but, by Jove, she was switched on – she knew *exactly* what Reader was up to.

Later that evening, he managed to collar me on my own and he was at it again. 'Send your mother back to Scotland, Sydney,' he said, with his arm draped securely around my shoulder, 'I'm going to make you a star.' So, there you have it, I could have been a star years ago if I'd only let the late Ralph Reader get hold of me.

I may have been ambitious but I was never *that* ambitious. But the sad thing is that there are plenty of waifs and strays who didn't come from the kind of good home that I was lucky to have and there are plenty of unscrupulous people who would get their claws into them.

Ralph's indecent proposal only made me more depressed and I pined for the days when Kathleen and I could enjoy our stolen moments again. Please don't get me wrong – this wasn't out of love, it was pure lust. Fortunately my groin's prayers were answered and the show's producers decided to take *Wild Grows the Heather* back out on tour again. I think my cry of 'Yippee!' could probably have been heard as far away as Bellside.

First we moved it to Golders Green Empire before finishing up in Bournemouth and, while we were away, Kathleen and I could play. What really amazed me was how much she was risking for our affair. It was incredibly dangerous for her and she stood to lose the lot. Maybe she liked that aspect of it – the danger. I honestly don't know. All I do know is she had a lot more to lose than I did – all I really risked was a thick ear from my mum. Kathleen could have easily lost her job and her marriage. And that was another thing – she was actually happily married. It's strange what will bring two seemingly incompatible people together. But, after *Wild Grows the Heather,* that was it between us and I never saw Kathleen again. It was just a case of goodbye and a kiss on the cheek – no tears, no correspondence, no phone numbers, not even a scrape of a pen was ever exchanged and quite simply I never saw her again. But she was certainly responsible for turning a fifteen-year-old wet-behind-the-ears boy from Bellside into a man.

Straight after the last night of that show, my mum and I returned to Scotland. I went back with my tail between my legs because I thought I'd made it and London would be where I was based forever. So, when I got back home, I had to deal with the stark reality that my dream had ended. You can imagine the contrast – down south I had been performing in front of massive audiences and living a grand lifestyle with glitzy parties and now here I was back to Bellside again. I think I've explained more than enough how much my home meant to me but, I have to confess, my first thought on arriving back home was 'Oh, shit!'

The truth is it took me a long time to adjust and I went through a whole year of total inactivity after the show folded. I just couldn't sing. The high-pitched voice was gone and the innocent young boy who had left Lanarkshire was now back with a new deep voice and his head well and truly turned for good. But more worryingly I just physically could not sing. I believe Aled Jones had the same problem after his voice broke. It's very dangerous to push it and you have to give it a good rest to let the vocal cords settle down. So I went back to work on farms here and there and I would help my father sell the petrol but that was really it.

Fortunately, during this time, to give myself something to do, I bought a guitar from McCormicks, in Cowcaddens, for fourteen guineas. I had to pay it up or, as we used to say, 'Half a crown down and change of address.' I wouldn't say I became an expert player in that year but I was certainly passable. There was a fella I worked on a farm with called Peter Lynch, who played accordion – about as well as I played the guitar! And another guy called Bead, also known locally as Bead Hill for some reason I could never work out, and Jimmy Nicol on the spoons. So with our various 'talents' we started a skiffle group, covering the Lonnie Donegan songs that were all the rage at the time. The beauty about skiffle was that it only took two chords and even *we* could handle that. We would practise regularly at Bead Hill's house and our first gig was at a Cleland Welfare dance. The stupid thing was that we only knew about five tunes so we just kept repeating the songs. I suppose we must have done all right – well, put it this way, no one said we were rotten.

Village life brings you back to reality very quickly. Folk in Bellside don't put up with any airs and graces – a spoon is a shovel to these guys. It didn't matter what I'd done or where I'd been, I was still Sydney Devine from Bellside and, odd as it might seem, even if I was depressed at first because all my big hopes had been crushed, that's what I truly loved about the place – the fact that living in a village means you'll never get big-headed.

5

THE SENSATIONAL SYD
AND ALEX BAND

In 1957, I was gigging here and there with my little band when, one day – I can't quite remember how it all came about – I did a concert for Anderson Boyd, an engineering firm in Craigneuk, Motherwell. I got up with the guitar and, for the first time in my life, I sang 'Singing the Blues'. At the time, Tommy Steele was at number one with the song.

After that, I entered a competition – as you'll have guessed by now, I liked entering competitions – to find Scotland's answer to Tommy Steele who was huge at the time. It was being run by the *Daily Record* and they were determined to find someone who could storm the charts and become a star like Tommy. I thought to myself, 'I can play the guitar, I can sing and I can whistle and I've already been knocking audiences dead with 'Singing the Blues' – I'll be a shoo-in.' So I entered this competition, thinking I was going to win it. I came second and I just couldn't believe it. In my own mind, I was convinced that I was home and dry. And you'll never guess who beat me – Alex Harvey who later went on to form The Sensational Alex Harvey Band but, back then, he was just plain Alex Harvey.

I actually went all round Scotland with Alex as the *Daily Record* sponsored a tour for the winner and the runner-up. I'd go onstage and sing 'Singing the Blues', Tommy Steele's very sedate hit. I'd slowly sing, 'Well, I never felt more like singing the blues . . .' and then Alex Harvey would burst onstage after me like a wild man. He was all energy, sex appeal and rock 'n' roll – the contrast between the two of us couldn't have been greater. There was no competition really. He was a big entertainer. To me, he was a classic rock 'n' roller and, sadly, in my opinion, he was never given the recognition he truly deserved.

I loved being on tour with him. I was only seventeen and we had a wild time – well, what else could you have with a wild man like Alex? We would play all of these little venues and the audiences had never seen anything like us in their lives – although I don't think they were too impressed by me. Here I was, a teenager, going onstage in my kilt. I'd look down at all these girls my own age and could see them smirking and thinking, 'What's going on here?' They wanted rock 'n' roll not 'A Gordon for Me'. But it actually set up Alex beautifully because, after I'd done my two spots, Alex would leap onstage and blow them away. However, at that time, Alex only knew about four or five songs and you couldn't do a whole show with somebody who only knew four or five songs so, in fact, they needed me to do my spot too.

Alex was a bit older than me and he and I may have been chalk and cheese but we got on great. He was an incredibly nice guy but touring with him was the only time I've ever lost money. Nobody had any money and I always had borrow cash from my mother. The tour was put on with typical newspaper organisation – half-ersed! We were so skint that, when we broke a guitar string, we had no other option but to tie it back together.

The *Record* had bought us an old taxi to travel about in and there were literally six or seven of us in the back of this ancient thing. We ate, drank and slept in it – in fact we did everything in it. We were all frisky young men so, of course, women were involved. They'd throw themselves at us – particularly Alex because he just had such incredible charisma. That and his huge musical talent were to bring him massive success four or five years later when he formed The Sensational Alex Harvey Band. Alex was up for anything in a skirt and he put that taxi's back seat to good use. As for the rest of us, well, without wanting to sound too coarse, we would watch what was going on and wait our turn . . .

The *Record* tour only lasted a few weeks and, after it finished, Alex and I did a load of dances in the Borders for a promoter called Duncan McKinnon. I remember Alex Harvey and I were in Carlisle one night and, as usual, we didn't have any money. We'd packed our instruments into the taxi so there wasn't room for all of us to sleep in it. Four of us would sleep in the cab, curled up under overcoats, and the others would have to go into the station in Carlisle and sleep in the waiting room which, back then, had coal fires. On this particular night, Alex and I drew the short straws and we shuffled off to the station. At two o'clock in the morning, I felt someone rapping me on the shoulder. A giant copper was standing over me, saying, 'Get out, please.' I said, 'I'm just waiting on my train.' 'Aye, well, wait outside, sonny,' the cop said. So Alex and I were thrown out on to the streets of Carlisle in the middle of night, freezing and with no money.

One time we were in Inverness and again we got to sleep with every girl in sight and we shared them too. We were playing a place called The Meeting Rooms and, afterwards, we were invited to this party by twin sisters. The only problem was that we had no music as our instruments were locked up in the venue. So our bass player, Charlie Carswell, who was

41

quite handy with his fists, said, 'We'll just f***ing break in to The Meeting Rooms and steal our own guitars.' So he did. And, to top it all, I think we later claimed the insurance on our 'stolen' guitars. But what a party! Not only did Alex and I sleep with both twins, I reckon the rest of the band did too. Talk about rock 'n' roll . . . It was just a wild, crazy time.

Strangely enough though, I didn't drink on tour. Well, we hardly had any money so it would have been a bit difficult. I didn't really start drinking until I was twenty-one. There was no drug-taking either – who needs drink and drugs when you've got groupies like that?

It was a weird set-up because, although every venue was absolutely mobbed, no one was getting paid and, to survive, I'd have to go home and tap my mother for money. It seemed like we toured for about twenty years but it was probably more like a year – but what an incredible time it was.

Another time, we were playing in Arbroath and, as usual, it was always my intention to play some rock 'n' roll as well as the hills-and-heather music that I was known for. In the first half, I'd wear the kilt and give them the traditional stuff and then, in the second half, I'd come out, dressed in a slick shirt and denim jeans, and give it laldy. The guitarist with Alex at that time was a little fella called Joe Moretti, who looked Italian and was a really handsome guy. Now Joe was a great guitarist but he never got the chance to sing as Alex was always there. But, this night, after a few glasses of wine, he started strumming and singing something I had never ever heard before. I said to Joe, 'What's that?' He told me it was a song by a guy called Hank Williams and he sang it again and again. That was my introduction to country music. Years later when I was recording a country album at Phonogram in London, Joe Moretti was the session guitarist. My producer Tommy Scott asked, 'Sydney, do you know Joe?' I looked at Tommy and said, 'Know him? This is the guy who introduced me to country music.'

Joe was from Glasgow's Gallowgate where his dad ran a coal delivery business and I always fancied his sister Pat like crazy. She was a dark-haired beauty, very exotic looking, and she would occasionally come to our gigs. One night, we ended up back at Joe's place and I remember trying it on with her. She was in another room on a pull-down bed and I crept through to see if she fancied getting up to anything – God loves a chancer. I can't recall exactly what happened but I heard a door slam and I couldn't get out of Pat's bed quick enough. The fear of being caught meant our relationship went unconsummated.

After our wild year touring, Alex and I went our separate ways and we lost contact. Although, funnily enough, in later years when I played at Glasgow's Pavilion Theatre, his father was the stage doorkeeper there. Les Harvey was a wonderful wee man – in fact, all the Harveys were great, a really nice family.

I knew Alex's brother Les too. Alex was a very good guitarist but Les was even better and the funny thing was that Alex had taught him to play. From about the age of nine, Les was just an incredible player and rock 'n' roll really was in that family's blood. In later years, he went off and formed a band called Stone the Crows with his girlfriend Maggie Bell – they were a fabulous rock group. I remember seeing them and thinking that they were probably one of the best groups I had heard in a long, long time. But then in 1972 tragedy stuck when Les was electrocuted at a gig in Swansea and died onstage, right in front of Maggie who was by now his fiancée. He was just twenty-five at the time and

I couldn't believe it – the wee guy who used to blow me away with his guitar playing was suddenly dead. It seemed so pointless. A waste. A real tragedy and I don't think Maggie ever recovered from it. It was just awful and I really felt for the Harveys. They were such a close family and I knew this would hit them harder than most. But then who would believe it? Tragedy of tragedies, ten years later, Alex died from a heart attack at a Belgian ferry terminal. They both had so much more to offer and their untimely deaths made me realise how cruel life can be.

But, for two fellas who had been so close on that *Daily Record* tour, our careers couldn't have taken more different paths. In 1959, I rejoined Robert Wilson's White Heather Group. So, while Alex was screaming into a microphone, I was giving it 'How's your maw for sugar?' and all the heedrum-hodrum stuff. But it wasn't so bad for me bearing in mind that I grew up with that genre and Robert Wilson was a hero in the Devine household.

When Robert asked me to come back, I was performing around the theatres with my guitar. He called and said that I should think about going on tour with him again as things were very different. He had Gordon McKenzie in the group, playing and singing Scottish music, along with Will Starr on accordion. But he didn't want me to join them. He offered me the chance to do rock 'n' roll and I jumped at it because that was exactly what I wanted to do. So he billed me as the Tartan Rocker and I toured the world with Robert for the next ten years.

Robert and The White Heather Group were surrounded by some incredible characters. One was Tammy Fisher who was a very good piano player. His other talent was that he could do the *Daily Express* crossword in about half an hour.

We were playing the Town Hall in Falkirk and, in those days, the stages had what was called a rake on them – a slant that went right down to the footlights. Now quite a few folk associated with The White Heather Group had massive drink problems and Tammy was one of them. This particular night Tammy had really hit the ale. His drinking never affected his performance – what he did on the piano was automatic because it was the same every night. Robert and the band's stint was about an hour long and they were on in the second half of the gig. Before they came on, Tammy had had maybe two pints too many and he was sitting at the piano absolutely bursting. Anyway, he got to the point where he couldn't hold it in any longer and there was nothing else for it – he wet himself on the stage. And, sitting behind the piano, he might have got away with it had it not been for the rake of the stage. As the pee streamed down to the footlights, one by one the lights all blew – ping, ping, ping . . .

Robert also had a reputation as a big boozer but I saw no evidence of it. I think he got the reputation when he had been invited to The Press Fund Ball back in the early 40s. He was the undisputed Voice of Scotland back then and was doing the cabaret that night. When someone told him he'd left the lights on his car – the massive flashy Austin Sheerline he had at the time – he'd probably had a couple of whiskies too many. So he went out, put the key in the door and the police nicked him. He was charged and done for being drunk in charge of a vehicle and the same people who had been filling him with booze then reported that he'd been done in all the papers. From that day on, he was always known as Wilson the drunkard. But I worked with him for ten years and I only saw him drunk once in my life – just once in ten years. He actually couldn't drink. He didn't have the stomach for it as he suffered from an ulcer or something which meant he had to take bicarb of soda about three or four times a day every day. But even though he couldn't drink, he was always, unjustly in my eyes, known as a big boozer.

Robert Wilson did, however, seem to have the knack of employing some quite heroic drinkers. Will Starr was phenomenal. He came from the mining village of Croy and he was a genius with a button accordion. For most of his life, Will had a chronic alcohol problem. There would be some nights where I've seen myself standing behind the front curtains holding on to Will's accordion straps to keep him upright. It got to the stage where we'd taken to searching him for half bottles of whisky before concerts as we tried in vain to keep him sober. He had various places for hiding them. He even used toilet cisterns – and I'm talking about the old-fashioned high-up ones with long chains. He'd do anything to plank his booze. Finally, when he'd run out of hiding places, fly Will started buying two half bottles. One was a sort of decoy and while we were searching for it, he'd be getting stuck in to the other one.

Probably his most ingenious hiding place was inside the bellows of the accordion itself. He'd take a small screwdriver and loosen the bellows and plank his bottle in there and it wouldn't actually make any difference to the sound it made when he played. Will was always such a really nice, genuine man. He'd call me 'the darling boy' but the drink was the most important thing in his life and, eventually, all that mattered to him was where his next one was coming from. There were occasions when Robert had to go and get his accordion out of a pawnshop before he could go onstage – it really had got that bad.

In the end, poor Robert was at his wits end and he paid for Will to go into a private clinic in Edinburgh to dry out. It cost Robert a lot of money but Will was in a really bad way and Robert desperately wanted to help him out. Of course, you can't really help an alcoholic or a drug addict until such times as they decide they need help themselves and sadly that was the case with Will. He must have spent about three weeks drying out at the clinic. On his first night back with us, we were at the Gaiety Theatre in Ayr and we couldn't believe it when Will staggered onstage. During the break, Robert asked him if he'd been drinking again but Will assured him he hadn't and it was the pills from the clinic that were affecting him. It was a good story but the truth is Will was absolutely fleeing on what was his first night out of the clinic.

I saw Will years and years later and the transformation was unbelievable. Somewhere along the line, he had decided he wasn't going to drink any more – as I said, alcoholics have to come to that conclusion themselves – and he had got his life back on track. He had a car, which is something he'd never had in his life before, a chequebook and rings on his fingers, which was also new as he used to pawn all his jewellery. He really had straightened himself out but then, after what must have been a huge battle to beat the booze, he was diagnosed with cancer. I went to see him in Belvidere Hospital and it was so sad that, after all the time he spent struggling with alcoholism, he only lived seven years before dying from cancer. He's a great loss to Scottish theatre and, even to this day, when people talk about accordionists, they still say that Will Starr was the best.

But Will's antics had their rivals. With a cast like ours, there was always something going on. One time, in Dundee, our piano player Terry O'Duffy had been out for his usual night on the bevvy. His room was on the fourth floor and the 'facilities' – you didn't have en suite rooms in the kind of places we frequented – were down on the ground floor. At about 3 o'clock in the morning, Terry needed the toilet and couldn't be bothered making the trek downstairs so he filled an empty ginger bottle instead. However, midway through emptying his bladder, he decided he needed more than just a pee. So he grabbed a newspaper and, like a puppy, he poo-ed on that. Of course, all this time, he was being watched by his roommate Billy Denniston. Billy called him a dirty little bastard and Terry begged him not to tell anybody.

Pros being pros, Billy couldn't get into the theatre quick enough the next morning to tell everybody. Halfway through rehearsals, Robert Wilson went over to Terry and said, 'You dirty little bastard, imagine doing a thing like that.' Terry was all embarrassed and asked Robert, 'Who told you?' Quick as a flash, Robert said, 'Nobody – I read it in the paper. They'll print any shite this weather!'

Incredibly, during all the time I was touring with Robert, I never once got back on television or radio. I just did the stage shows. We were The White Heather Group and our rivals, The White Heather Club, were controlled by the BBC and a man called Ian McFadyen. Now, for some reason known only to himself, Ian didn't like me and, if someone at the BBC doesn't like you, you've no chance of getting in there. So, for a decade, I was basically blacklisted and I never, to this day, found out why. Ian is dead and gone now but he denied me the chance of advancement during that early period of my career. I knew I was capable of doing television and he gave slots to groups like The Joe Gordon Folk Four and everyone else in The White Heather Group but he wouldn't touch me with a bargepole.

Normally, in this business, you get a hint of why someone doesn't like you but I heard nothing, not even a hint, as to why he had taken against me. I could never understand it but I guess he just didn't like me. It was so frustrating as he came to watch The White Heather Group many, many times and it even seemed like he enjoyed booking everyone else around me for the telly and deliberately leaving me out. The rest of the group felt sorry for me but there was no way they could turn him down as they had their own careers to think about. So, for ten whole years, I went without telly and radio appearances and just plugged away at the stage shows. I was stuck in a rut and I knew it but I was making a living so at least that was something.

The White Heather Group were also invited to tour Canada and I wasn't included on that either. This was because a man called Neil Kirk, who was a Canadian impresario, didn't rate me. He just didn't think that what I was doing fitted the taste of the times and he wanted to play it safe. His decision effectively ended any hopes I had of breaking into that vast market over there. So, between them, these two men managed to set my career back years.

Despite these setbacks, I enjoyed my time with Robert Wilson. He was the world's worst explorer and he would take us to places I don't think even Hillary had been to – I kid you not. I was finding myself back in all these wee places I'd played as a youngster but, to be honest, I don't think they were really ready for a Tartan Rocker. When we played places like Orkney, Shetland and many of the other islands, the audiences were expecting to see Robert Wilson and The White Heather Group. But what they got as well was me with a guitar and an amplifier. I'd begin with 'When I was just a little boy . . .' before bursting into 'You ain't nothing but a hound dog' – they certainly weren't expecting that. It was hard for me in those days singing rock 'n' roll to folk like the Shetland Islanders. However, the chances were, when I played any venue, there would usually be a section of the crowd who liked the rockier stuff and, eventually, more and more got into what I was doing.

But, even though I was rocking 'n' rolling onstage, I certainly wasn't living the rock-'n'-roll lifestyle offstage. Being on tour with The White Heather Group was very sedate compared to those incredibly wild times out on the road with Alex Harvey. So things calmed down, everything kind of went back to normal and there were no more mad parties or any of that. There were still plenty of girls who were always waiting for me at the stage door but I quickly learned that, when some girl comes to the stage door looking for autographs, it's never a good idea to start dating them afterwards. You lose a fan for a start off and it can be a dangerous road to go down as, who knows, it could even lead to marriage . . .

6

MEETING SHIRLEY

Now, even though I said going out with a fan was dangerous territory, that was how I actually met Shirley. She was to become the first woman I'd ever had a proper relationship with and she's the woman I'm still married to, to this day. I was performing at the Tivoli Theatre in Aberdeen where, once a week, every week, Shirley was a member of the audience. She had a front-row seat for every show so, winter season or summer season, there she was.

After one show, I decided to give her a wink and she came round to the stage door for an autograph and that was it. I was eighteen and Shirley was twenty. We kept our long-distance relationship going with loads of letters – phone calls weren't that easy in those days as most people didn't have home phones and it meant using telephone boxes. What was different about Shirley? I honestly don't know – somewhere inside me, I just knew that she was the girl for me. However, although I kept in touch with Shirley, as far I was concerned, there was no concrete commitment between us and I was still footloose and fancy free.

I was still sowing my wild oats all over Scotland and seemed to have girls in every port. I'm not writing about this because I'm some sort of braggart – I was never into kiss-and-tells. This was just the reality of being a young singer out on the road and what I experienced was probably no different from what every other young singer or band member was going through at the time. I was also never the type to count the number of notches on my bedpost and I wouldn't even like to try. Put it this way, I was desperate to ease up a bit as it was all getting too much. Sex was everywhere I went. If it wasn't a fan, then it was someone from the cast. As I said, I'm not telling tales out of school and I think if you try to put a figure to it, it just looks like you're boasting – but I'm not. This was just how it was. There was never any scarcity. Eventually, I decided I had had enough as I could have been at it every day if I wanted to. But it's like a nice hot bath – it's not so hot once you're used to it. Something that is so readily available suddenly becomes not as desirable even though you'd imagine, when I was young, I wouldn't be thinking along those lines – but, believe me, I did. It was undoubtedly an interesting, but very exhausting, time of my life. Despite what I was getting up to, there would always be Shirley in the background and, whenever I returned home to my parents' house, there would be a letter from her waiting for me.

In Aberdeen, Shirley was a local beauty queen – she'd won something like twenty-three beauty contests. She was working for a company in Aberdeen called Esslemont and Macintosh. It was a big department store, Aberdeen's equivalent of Edinburgh's Jenners, and she worked as an operator of a post machine. She lived in the country as her father was a farmer so she used to travel in to the city every day.

We had kept our long-distance romance going for about two years when, one day in September, I just decided to propose. I had been away playing the American military bases in Germany with The White Heather Group. It was my first time abroad and I think I was pretty depressed about a lot of things that happened when I was over there. They were hard gigs and, again I'm not trying to be boastful, but I lost count how many times I had to pull them out of a hole. Professionally, Germany was a great learning curve for me as I quickly had to work out what the punters wanted. We actually had to do a showcase for all the booking agents before they sent us out to the bases. We'd arrive at a venue and there would be three or four other acts all competing for the job and we'd be asked to do a full set in front of the bookers. We all went through our entire routines and I reckon, if I hadn't been there, The White Heather Group wouldn't have picked up any bookings. These big, fat American agents just kept saying, 'Who are these guys in the skirts?' Most of the troops we would be playing for were black guys and what they wanted was rock 'n' roll. They didn't want to hear about the hills and the bonnie blooming heather and I was the only one on the tour who could supply something they could get into.

One night, we arrived in Freidberg and, lo and behold, my hero Elvis Presley was there at the time but I never found this out until after the show. While I was packing away the gear, the commanding officer of the base came up to me and said, 'Mr Presley has been in watching you.' That was all he said so I never discovered if he thought I was good, bad or indifferent. But, frankly, who cares? The King had actually been in there watching me singing *his* songs. If I'd known beforehand, I don't think I would have been able to go through with the show. This guy was the biggest star in the world and here I was doing 'Heartbreak Hotel', 'Hound Dog' and 'Blue Suede Shoes'. I just about went through his whole repertoire and, little did I know it, The King himself was tucked away in a corner, watching some boy from Scotland imitate him – incredible! Years later, I would find myself in the presence of Elvis again but that's a different story and one that is a lot more scary.

On tour with me in Germany was a guy called Billy Crotchet, who's passed away now, and this girl called Jeannie, who was from Sheffield. We just called her Jeannie Crotchet although I don't think they were married. Jeannie was the most gorgeous-looking girl, with the most fantastic figure I'd ever seen – and I'd seen a lot of girls – but, sadly, she wasn't too bright. Billy had originally started out as a clown before going into music hall comedy. That was where he met Jeannie and he toured around with her as his assistant and the pair of them lived in a caravan together. Billy was a bald-headed, skelly-eyed wee guy and I could never figure out for the life of me why an attractive young girl like Jeannie was with him. The world is a certainly strange place but even stranger was the fact that she never left him because it was no secret that he used to knock hell out of her. Now I have always firmly believed that no one is allowed to hit a woman but they had such a fiery relationship that I sometimes think she deliberately goaded him into it. It was all very, very weird.

One night, we were in this pretty rough hotel in a place called Mannheim. The hotel was where all the pros playing the bases in that area would stay. It was our night off and we'd all gone out and got sloshed. Crotchet and Jeannie were in the room next door to mine and, not long after we got back, I heard it all start – the punches being thrown, the screams and the crying. I got out of bed, knocked on their door and said, 'I'm trying to get to sleep – keep it down.' Five minutes later, it all kicked off again and, this time, she was crying even louder. So I banged on the door and said, 'Don't have me getting up again.'

No sooner had my head touched the pillow than they were at it again. This time I really thumped their door, only for it to fly open. Billy swung a punch at me but I managed to duck just in time. When I came up, I caught him with a punch right on his chin and knocked him over. I said to him, if he wanted to fight, he should try someone his own size and I told him to get up and get outside. I stormed outside and I was ready to hammer this woman-beating bastard. Crotchet followed behind me and I pinned him up against the wall of the hotel. He said, 'Go on, hit me if that's what you want to do.' This threw me slightly – I couldn't hit someone who wasn't prepared to defend himself – so I told him he was pathetic and turned around to go back to my bed when suddenly the little bastard booted me in the back. I swung round and I gave him a right going-over – it really was one of the worst things I've ever done in my life. I punched him, kicked him and jumped on top of him. It was horrible and it makes me sick to the pit of my stomach to think that I actually did that to another human being but that wee man really did manage to bring out the worst in folk.

As I was laying into Crochet, our little piano player Terry O'Duffy – the one who couldn't be bothered to take himself off to the toilet and had used a newspaper instead – was returning from a night on the sauce. Terry's real name was Terry Redmond and he stayed in Cumberland Street in the Gorbals. He used to perform with his brother Eugene – Terry at the piano and Eugene on the violin – and they called themselves The Redmond Brothers. Everyone else called them The Red Wine Brothers which was self-explanatory really. In fact, Terry used to put a bottle of red wine into his coat pocket and hang it on the back of the dressing room door. Every so often, he'd go up to his coat, uncork the bottle and take a slug without taking the wine out of his coat pocket – he was quite a character.

Anyway, Terry had been out on the batter and he was staggering along the street when he saw me laying into Crochet. Terry hated Billy so suddenly there were two of us putting the boot in. As I said, this strange wee man really did have an uncanny knack of bringing out the absolute worst in people. This unsavoury incident kind of put the tin lid on the whole Germany trip for me and I really began to hate the entire tour.

I think the going-over I gave Crochet that night was the result of a lot of pent-up rage. Before that night, he'd constantly been niggling me and the rest of The White Heather Group. The ironic thing was that what he was doing in the show didn't mean anything to these GIs in Germany. When we performed in Scotland, he was actually a very funny man with a good act and he was an integral part of The White Heather Group. But, over in Germany, he was dying on his arse. Meanwhile, I was getting a great reception at the gigs – well, who could fail with rock 'n' roll? This started to play on Billy's mind and that was why he was always niggling and tossing out little barbed comments here and there. I don't know why it bothered him so much. My attitude was that we were all one big team. If my act wasn't going down well, I'd hope someone else would be able to pull me out of the hole. I believed that, as long we were working, that was the most important thing. But Billy didn't share this outlook. His view was that, if he wasn't having a good time, he wanted to make sure the rest of us weren't enjoying ourselves either. I didn't like working under these circumstances. I didn't like this weird little man who could bring out the worst in me but sometimes, I guess, you have to fight for your livelihood.

Although I hated this wretched German tour, it did have its lighter moments. Terry Redmond and I were sharing a room and Terry was renowned for being built like a horse – and here I'm referring to between his legs. Anyway, one night at about three in the morning, Terry came in with this German dame while I was sleeping. The room was so small that the only way to fit two beds in was to have them head to toe. So Terry and the woman were trying to be as quiet as possible but, despite their attempts at keeping the noise down, I was soon wide awake. They were both doing what comes naturally and going at it hammer and tongs – a real rampant job – and I couldn't help but see and hear everything. Anyway, after they're finished, the dame decided to go to the wash-hand basin and give herself a wash – and I'm not talking about her face here. She grabbed my bottle of Old Spice aftershave from the shelf, obviously thinking it was soap, and splashed it on down below. Suddenly, she screamed, 'My pussy's kaput!' She made a quick exit after that but she left behind an image I will never forget as long as I live of a huge, naked Fräulein running around that hotel room, shouting, 'My pussy's kaput!'

Sadly, the pussy's kaput incident was one of the few highlights of the entire trip and, after my bust-up with Crochet, I phoned Shirley from Germany and asked, 'What are you doing on the eleventh of November?' Shirley said, 'I don't know – it's a long way off.' So I told her, 'Well, keep it free because we're getting married.' And that was that.

I made the call on the spur of the moment and it was probably prompted by everything that had happened. Bear in mind I was only twenty years old at the time and was in a foreign country. I wasn't living in the best conditions. Also, I was part of a show that was struggling every night and the pressure was really on me to pull the rest of them through. It really was an ill-fated and bad-tempered affair and suddenly, during all the shit that was going on, I had this moment of clarity when I just knew that the one person I wanted to be with for the rest of my life was Shirley.

The truth was that Shirley and her friend Eleanor, who was to her bridesmaid, were regulars at Aberdeen's Tivoli Theatre and they really didn't care too much who they came to see. They simply loved the theatre and always made sure they had their same front-row seats, where I'd spotted her time and time again before deciding to give her the wink – the famous Devine wink no less! And Shirley always maintains that I only proposed to her from Germany because she was threatening to go off with someone else. There's also a wee bit of debate about how I did ask her to marry me – she still insists that she read about it in the newspaper before I called her – well, I like to give a woman time to prepare herself. She says she was at work when her boss came through and said, 'The *Press and Journal* are on the phone – they want a statement about your impending marriage to Sydney Devine.' I may or may not have phoned Jackie Cruickshank, a journalist friend in Inverness who wrote for the *Press and Journal's* Inverness edition at the time, to tell him what I was going to do. Even though I wasn't a big name or anything like that, it was fairly big news for them – I was in showbiz and I was marrying one of their local beauty queens. However, I gather her mother was none too pleased when a reporter arrived at her door looking for a statement.

Although we may have been fairly big news up in Aberdeen, not everyone looked upon our union favourably. Shirley has always been a church-going person but, when she tried to make arrangements for our marriage at the West Church in

Inverurie, the minister, Colin McPherson, refused to marry us because he said that I never attended his services. And, as if that wasn't bad enough, Mr McPherson, in his infinite wisdom and high up on his moral pedestal, then told Shirley, 'I'll give you six months with that guy. Don't do it – you're too nice a person to get married to the likes of him.' We've been together for around forty-five years now so stick that in your pipe Mr McPherson. And the church wonders why attendances have plummeted over the years . . .

The first time I met Shirley's folks was quite eventful – it was just like *Meet the Fockers*. Her mum thought she'd impress me by making a ham salad. I was half way through it when all of a sudden there was a shout from Shirley's father in the kitchen, 'Jesus Christ, Mother, you've given that loon bacon instead of ham!' And she had. I'd been sitting munching raw bacon. I knew it was raw of course but I didn't dare say anything as it was my first meeting with them and I just thought, 'Well, maybe that's what they eat up here.' But, believe me, I've always taken my bacon crispy ever since.

I have to say, though, that Shirley's parents were delighted that we were marrying but the same could not be said of my own mother, who was very unhappy to say the least. Bear in mind I was her youngest, her baby, and she didn't want me to lose me so it could have been Princess Margaret I was marrying and she still wouldn't have been good enough for her boy. But, as is usually the case, when we did marry on the 11th of November 1961, it was a glorious wedding and everyone had a great time.

We only had a four-day honeymoon at my cousin Jeannie Donald's house in Trottick, in Dundee, before I was off for a month's tour of New Zealand and Australia. It was a trip that I very nearly didn't come back from . . .

7

AMAZING GRACE

Now occasionally, when I wasn't working with The White Heather Group – say, when they were away touring Canada without me – I would join the Bobby McLeod Tour, another bunch of entertainers that had more than its fair share of bampots and characters but, having said that, it was quite a cast. The boys in Bobby McLeod's band included accordionist Hugh Malarkey from Rothesay, bass player Fred McDougall, who was also from Rothesay, and the Perth piano player Pamela Brough. Again, it was quite difficult for me to slot in because it was a Scottish show and I was trying to do stuff like 'Singing the Blues' and 'Jailhouse Rock'. If I could perform popular songs, as opposed to Scottish ones, and survive, I considered that night's performance to have been a success.

Also in the group was also a fella called Walter Jackson, a comedian who did impersonations of Lou Costello. His real name was actually Wolfgang Jacobsen from Giffnock – you can see why he changed his name as growing up in Giffnock called Wolfgang must have been hazardous. I never knew if Walter was gay or just a big mammy's boy but he was always sooking up to folk, especially if they were in a position of power. He was such a brown-nose, I'm surprised anyone employed him.

In the VW minibus that took the cast from venue to venue, Bobby McLeod, Hugh Malarkey and Fen (full name

Fenwick) McDougall had a great way of speaking. It was called the McFarlane and Lang which stands for slang. So it was Scottish slang – like Cockney rhyming slang but better. So, your *strip Jack naiket* was your jaiket (jacket), your *Edinburgh rock*, well, that was a man's you-know-what and Seterday Sanny was a character in one of the Scottish newspapers but, to them, it rhymed perfectly with a slang word for a lady's private parts. Of course, being young, I was fascinated by all this. To begin with, they could hold whole conversations and I wouldn't know what they were talking about but I soon picked it up and I remember most of it to this day. It got quite advanced and often two and three word phrases were reduced to just one word and you could fill the rest in yourself. So, in, for example, 'There's the Harry', Harry was short for Harry Margolis (a Glasgow-based entertainment agency) and it meant the polis. There was a word for everything so you could have a complete conversation. When others were trying to learn, sometimes they screwed up big time and the three of them would just take the hit and miss out you when you got it wrong!

On that tour, there was a girl called Anna Cowie. She was a piano player who performed for the rest of the acts on the bill. Although she didn't play too well, she became known as Anna the Piana or Fingers Cowie. You could say that her right hand had fallen out with her left hand years ago and they just refused to make up! One of her friends was Grace Logan, who was married to Jimmy Logan. At one time, she had been a dancer at the old Metropole and that was where she met Jimmy. Being a young man who quite fancied older women, I fell head over heels for Grace. She was probably the first person I had a real serious crush on. She was a married woman by then – although that never stopped me in *Wild Grows the Heather* – and I'd only see her when she came to keep her pal Anna Cowie company on the tour. It was torture being in her company because she was stunning and so well turned out. I never made my feelings known but she wasn't stupid and would have easily been able to spot the teenager who was fascinated by her.

For almost three weeks I was in her company every day and the one good thing about having her on board was that she taught me to dance. Each day, she'd put me through my paces and show me how to do the Elvis Presley moves – the leg shakes and what have you – which put me in such good stead throughout my career.

In later years, when I was taking short breaks from The White Heather Group, I went to work with the Prince of the Highlands – Mr Calum Kennedy – and I soon discovered he had a bit of a reputation for not paying wages. The stories about Calum are legendary. The one time I toured with him, Chic Murray was with us too, albeit in his twilight years – two of the tightest men on the planet on the same bill. Normally, when a show was finished, we'd have a drink in the bar but it would become quite obvious that Chic wasn't buying any drink. Now, Chic was renowned for that old trick but, because of who he was, everyone just seemed to let him get away with it. Towards the end of our tour, we were in a little hotel in Campbeltown and Chic was propping up the bar as usual. Everyone was buying rounds except Chic although he was knocking drinks back left, right and centre. So I went to get a round in and said, 'Same again, barman – large ones this time.' Chic turned to me and said, 'That's very kind of you, Syd.' And I replied, 'No, that's kind of you – it's your round. You've been drinking for a fortnight and haven't bought a drink for anyone.' He seemed quite embarrassed that'd I'd brought it up – especially as I had spoken so loudly the whole hotel heard it. He paid up in front of everyone, with a degree of mock hurt. However, I think old Chic had a very thick skin and would have been neither here nor there about it – after all what's a few minutes of discomfort when you've been drinking for free for weeks?

But, if it wasn't Chic's meanness I had to deal with, it was Calum's. I remember being in Arbroath and I was waiting on my wages to go home and Calum said, 'I'll send them on to you, Sydney' but, knowing his reputation, I insisted that I'd wait for my wages. After a while, he reluctantly handed over what I was due but he was quite a character – especially when it came to money matters. Calum was great company and told some fantastic stories from his years on tour. He told me once how he toured the pantomime, *Cinderella*. When you think about it, taking an entire production round the country – from Dundee to Orkney and the whole of the Highlands – in the middle of winter was quite a feat. Calum played Prince Charming of the Highlands. The cast included Will Hannah Jr, another accordionist who liked a little libation, Sheikh Ben Ali, a magician, and Jimmy Fletcher, a wee fella from Fife who did a man in the suitcase routine.

One night they were playing in Inverness and, in the middle of the second half, they lost the bell that was used to count down the chimes to midnight when Cinderella changed back into her rags. Anyway, Calum came up with the idea of a stagehand using a glass and a spoon held up to the microphone. It was doing the trick 'ding, ding, ding' when suddenly there was a smash. The bloody glass had broken and then all the audience heard was the stagehand going, 'Seven, eight, nine, ten, eleven, twelve.' Seemingly, the whole place just erupted in fits of laughter.

But these other tours were just one-offs. For the most part, I was in with the bricks and mortar of The White Heather Group – or so I thought . . .

8

DOWN UNDER

It took thirty-two horrific hours on a plane to get to New Zealand for the first leg of our tour. We were playing in Auckland, Wellington, Napier, Hamilton, Dunedin, Invercargill – all the major towns and cities. We even made an album in the Town Hall in Wellington, with our huge cast which included Aileen Manson, the accordionist, Isabel James the dancer who's now married to the Scottish comedian and playwright Tony Roper, Jimmy Shand Jr, The Joe Gordon Folk Four, my good old pal Billy Crotchet and, of course, his long-suffering partner Jeannie, Terry O'Duffy, myself and Robert Wilson, leading from the front as usual.

Even though it was probably the twilight of Robert Wilson's career, we did extremely well and it was a pretty big deal when we rolled into town. The expats didn't seem to care and he was still a big name to them. But, although the crowds were huge and very receptive, I couldn't help being touched by sadness at the plight of most of the expats because many would never, ever go home again as they couldn't afford the air fare. I got to meet lots of expats after shows when they queued up for autographs or when I posed for pictures with the various Scottish societies. Almost every single one of them had gone to New Zealand on the £10 assisted package, which was a great idea to get people out of horrible poverty back home and give them a new start but it did mean that they were stuck there forever.

So all you had to do was sing one chorus of 'Granny's Heilan' Hame' and you were nearly having to do the breaststroke to get out of the hall. They'd be in floods of tears and I felt heart sorry for them. When I looked down from the stage at all those tear-stained faces, I knew the sadness that was in their hearts and I would feel like greetin' too.

From New Zealand, we went to Australia where we actually played in some of the rugby stadiums, in front of 4,000 to 5,000 fans – that's how many tickets we were selling.

One day, before a show up near Brisbane, a bunch of us went for a hike. There was Jimmy Shand Jr, Bernie O'Connor, who was the bass player from The Joe Gordon Folk Four, Barry, our bus driver, and me. It was a roasting hot afternoon and, when we came to a big wide river, we decided to swim across it to get back to our hotel as we didn't fancy walking three miles downstream again to cross on the bridge. Anyway, about halfway across the river, Jimmy Shand Jr started to lose it. He was panicking big style and, instead of carrying on, he decided he had to swim back to the shore we'd come from. Even though he'd taken a panic attack, I still didn't fancy aborting our mission and trudging all the way to the bridge so I said to Jimmy Shand Jr, 'I'll tell you what we'll do – Barry goes in the front, I'll go at the back and you can swim in between us and that way we can look after you.'

It seemed like a good idea at the time but we got about three quarters of the way over this time when Jimmy started to tread water. I swam up beside him to offer some words of encouragement – like 'Move your arse!' – and he grabbed me with incredible force around my neck and pulled me under. Now I've heard stories before about how you should avoid getting too close to people who are drowning as they can drown you too and I don't know if I truly believed it. But here I was, under the water, fighting for breath and I swear that my whole life flashed before my eyes and I'm not just saying that as an expression. I really do mean that it literally flashed before my eyes – images of my mother, father, the first day I went to school – and everything as clear as day.

Jimmy eventually let me go and never has the air rushing into my lungs felt sweeter. But I had just managed to get a couple of breaths in when he went and did it again and, this time, I started to panic too. Fortunately Barry, the bus driver, turned round and saw what was going on and he managed to pull Jimmy off me and then, between the two of us, we dragged him coughing and spluttering to the side. It was the nearest thing to death that I had ever come to and to try to explain how it feels is impossibile. Even years later, when I went through heart surgery, I never felt the way I did the day that Jimmy Shand Jr tried to drown me.

Now I was never Jimmy's closest friend but he still has never apologised for that incident or even acknowledged the fact that I helped save his life. I always thought Jimmy was a bit of a weirdo. His favourite phrase was, 'Trust me.' Someone who has to keep telling you to trust them is the last person in the world you should actually trust. He would do strange things like hide in the girls' dressing rooms before they came in and then jump out and frighten them. I'm not, for a second, suggesting he was getting his kicks from that but I'd have rather chatted up the chorus line and try to bed them than give them frights – very strange man. So, whether he was embarrassed about nearly killing me or what, I just don't know. But he certainly never mentioned it although it was so traumatic I can remember the entire incident as clear as day.

In Australia, we were working for an Aberdonian guy called George Mennie, whose business was G. Mennie

Enterprises. George didn't have much of a clue when it came to organising a tour and he had us travelling north to Brisbane after the Christmas period. Now Brisbane in January would be about 110 degrees in the shade and we were covering thousands of miles to play in places like Townsville, Mackay and Cairns. Anyway, to take us up to these places, George Mennie – or Meanie as we rechristened him – hired a train but, believe me, this was not a luxurious mode of transport. It was a rickety old thing and, of course, in the height of the Australian summer, it was as hot as a baker's oven. To top it all, the toilet wasn't working so the whole journey was a hot, sticky nightmare.

However, once again, we met some really fantastic expats up in those far-flung places and they all received us with open arms. So, although I might moan about things like horrible train journeys, I still loved the whole adventure. I was seeing a different part of the world and, what's more, I was being paid to be there. As I've said, money doesn't motivate me – and I do mean that sincerely – but there is no way, as a young man just in his twenties, I could have afforded to travel so far and seen so much if it hadn't been for work.

But, despite all that and even though the shows were going incredibly well – night and day compared to Germany – I was desperate to get back home to my new wife.

9

UNLUCKY WHITE HEATHER

On December the 30th 1960, Shirley had given birth to our first child at the Simpson Memorial Pavilion in Edinburgh. At the time, I was with The White Heather Group, doing the winter season at the Empire Theatre in Inverness. When I heard the news, Desmond Carroll, a dancer in our show, and I went out and wet the baby's head big time. Not only was it Hogmanay, my first son had just been born – I think I can just about remember getting to bed that night!

Our daughter Karen was born on March the 12th 1964 at Belvidere Hospital in Glasgow. We were living in Shawlands then and I remember Shirley prodding me awake and saying, 'Syd, you'll have to take me to the hospital – the baby's coming!' Like a typical man, I just said, 'Let me give you a cuddle and you'll be OK.' Shirley's response to that left me in no doubt that we really did need to go so I got up and, later that day, Karen Shirley made her first appearance in the world.

I worked with The White Heather Group for ten years and it offered me the security a dad of two young children needed. But my safe little world was to be turned on its head when Robert Wilson was involved in a car accident. Ironically, Robert was going from his home in Ayr along the then notorious A77 to attend a funeral in Glasgow. It was such a bad smash that Robert never truly recovered from it and it was really the beginning of the end for The White Heather Group.

It was a terrible shock that a man who had been so inspirational in my entire career, from when I was practically a child, had been seriously hurt but I also had to cope with the fact that my sheltered existence had been shattered. Working for The White Heather Group meant that everything was done for me. We may not have stayed in the most luxurious surroundings out on the road but they were always booked and ready for us. Suddenly I was being tossed out into the real world as a solo act – something I hadn't been for a decade – and I had now to negotiate with agents, bookers, theatre bosses, you name it. And then, of course, there was the nitty-gritty of reserving accommodation. It was only when I had to do all that I realised just how well Robert had looked after us and seen to all the practicalities of touring. He'd sheltered us from all of that and we'd never once had to worry where our next gig or pay cheque were coming from.

Without the might and pulling power of the well-established White Heather Group behind me, I was now at the mercy of a company in Glasgow called W. R. Gault, the entertainment agents who basically had the monopoly in Scotland. If W. R. Gault at 13 Sauchiehall Street didn't use you, you didn't work – it was as simple as that. Not only were they the top agents, they also owned many of the theatres like The Pavilion and The Metropole in Glasgow and The Tivoli in Aberdeen. This meant that as well as charging you commission when they booked you to play one of their theatres, they were also charging you commission as your agent – so they had two bites at your income. But there was little choice – as I said, as you either worked for them at their price or you just didn't work at all in Scotland.

One of the agents for W. R. Gault was the owner's son Resting – honestly, his name really was Resting Gault which was ironic considering half their clients were always resting. Another was a woman called Nellie Sutherland whose teeth constantly chattered. Now, at Gault's, you had to climb a flight of stairs and go in the door to a little window that was like a serving hatch. Sometimes you'd go up there and Nellie would lift up the window, see who it was and BANG, she'd slam it shut again without saying a word to you. When that happened, it wasn't difficult to figure out there were no gigs for you that weekend.

There was a guy on their books who did a balancing act on a high wire. One day, he turned up and asked Nellie, 'Anything today?' And she said, 'No, nothing, son.' 'What about The Pavilion?' he asked. 'It's booked.' 'The Tivoli?' 'It's booked.' 'What about the Palladium in Edinburgh?' 'Booked, son, they're all booked.' 'What about Paisley, then?' Nellie replied, 'Your pole's too big for Paisley, son.' That's a line that has always stuck with me.

Ironically, I did do a couple of weekends for W. R. Gault at Paisley Theatre but, after that, I realised, if I wanted to get enough work, it definitely wasn't going to be in Scotland. I decided I'd have to get myself down to the working men's clubs in South Yorkshire and, as I faced this period of uncertainty, I came to appreciate what a huge and enjoyable part in my life The White Heather Group had played.

The last album we all recorded together was at the Albert Hall and it was titled simply *The White Heather Group at the Albert Hall*. I had a few of songs on it, including 'Jailhouse Rock', 'When the Saints Go Marching In' and 'Barnyards of Delgaty', which is what we call a bothy ballad. Robert wanted me to get into the bothy ballads because, by that time, The Joe Gordon Folk Four were doing so well with their Scottish bothy ballad folk songs.

During this time, I also started to think back fondly at all those years staying in some of the dodgiest accommodation on the planet. Because our mealtimes were irregular to say the least, we were always in places that catered solely for people in the theatrical profession. You couldn't have a meal in the early evening because you would be heading for the theatre not long after eating and there's nothing worse than going onstage and singing on a full stomach – it just can't be done. So, invariably, you had a supper as opposed to a tea or dinner. There was one woman in Carlisle who was a stickler for when meals were served – breakfast was from half past eight to quarter to nine, lunch was from one o'clock until quarter past and supper from ten thirty to eleven o'clock at night. The rigid times for breakfast weren't too bad and the lunch and supper times were fine under normal circumstances but sometimes, if rehearsals or the shows were running late, you couldn't get out in time. Her mealtimes often meant that I couldn't even nip in for half a pint of beer on the way back and I literally do mean a half pint because I couldn't afford anything else as, although the money was steady, it was never great.

One lunchtime, we didn't get back to this old battle-axe's until twenty past one – five minutes past her serving time – and she didn't appear. Eventually, I went through, knocked on the kitchen door and asked, 'Are we having lunch?' She curtly replied, 'Lunch is at one o'clock until quarter past' and that was it. So that Friday afternoon we went without our lunch. However, first thing on the Saturday morning, I went to the fish shop and bought a kipper. After we had our final lunch that day, I took a drawing pin, secured the fish underneath the table and just left. I don't know how long it took her to find that fish but I hope it had rotted and stank her house out. It may have been puerile and vengeful but that small victory felt very sweet to me.

Not only had The White Heather Group provided for me, it had also practically taught me everything I needed to know. For example, during my first stint with them, I spent a summer season performing at the Town Hall in Port Rush, Northern Ireland. I learned more about the theatrical profession in that one season than I ever did anywhere else. You had to change your act once every week so it gave you a bigger repertoire as you were constantly having to learn new stuff. I also had lots of other chores like going up to the lighting box, switching off the house lights and putting on the stage lights. I'd have to pull the curtains apart in time for the opening song and then quickly nip round the back and join the cast for a sing-a-long. And I'd have to slip offstage early to bring the curtains down. As well as doing my act, operating lights and opening and closing the curtain, during the interval I was out selling photographs for Robert Wilson. I turned my hand to everything and it was a fantastic experience for a young boy. At Port Rush, I met up with the ventriloquist Ken Swan and his dummy Magee again and he worked with us for the season. Ventriloquists are a weird bunch. I have yet to meet a ventriloquist who, if you go into their dressing room and their dummy is sitting on its box, can't resist throwing their voice. Ken was unique amongst ventriloquists, though, because his lips moved. He was a lovely fellow – just not the best ventriloquist I've seen.

Ken and I used to go swimming together during the heatwave in the summer of 1953. We'd use a diving board down at the harbour in Port Rush and its highest platform was thirty-three feet off the ground. That didn't bother Ken – he was a great diver and a very strong swimmer too. I was much more cautious and would never venture up to the top board. But, one day, Ken said to me, 'If you manage to dive off the highest board before the season finishes, I'll give you ten bob.' Now ten bob was equivalent to about ten quid nowadays and, eventually, I did it and managed to dive off the top board. Ken gladly gave me the money but his wife – an absolute battle-axe who treated every penny as a prisoner – was furious and she hated me from that day on. I can't remember the old bat's name – we just called her The Dragon and she deserved it for her reaction that day alone. Imagine behaving like that just because a thirteen-year-old had won a bit of money fair and square!

But, although I was having a great summer, swimming, winning bets and making a lifelong enemy of the ventriloquist's missus, the heatwave was killing the show – no one wanted to sit inside a hot stuffy theatre. The first house maybe only had about ten people who'd booked and sometimes there were more people on the stage than in the audience. Robert told us all not to worry about the first house as we'd do well at the second house. But no one was coming to see that show either – it was just too hot. Robert must have taken quite a hit financially during the long hot summer of 1953 but I guess that's showbiz.

I may have learned a lot with The White Heather Group but now, starting out as a solo entertainer, I was about to take one helluva crash course in showbiz.

10

GOING SOLO

So there I was – on my own for the first time in years. The White Heather Group was gone, I had a young son, Gary, a even younger daughter, Karen, and a concerned wife. We were living on the top floor of a tenement at 10 Ellangowan Road in Shawlands, Glasgow, and the money had dried up. There were only dribs and drabs of work available on my home patch and occasionally I'd play the likes of the Palace Bingo over in the Gorbals.

That's when I decided to head to Yorkshire and start playing the clubs in Sheffield. We had even made plans to move the family down south as I thought it was stupid to have a place in Scotland when most of my work was going to be in England. We had given up the flat in Shawlands and, while I was down in Sheffield working, I was looking for a place for us to live. One afternoon, I was driving out of a side street on to a main road when this bus cut the corner and ploughed right into me. The moment before impact, I remember thinking, 'I'm in deep shit here!' and I was right. I was quite badly hurt and my Ford Cortina was a write-off. I was in a right state and, later, I had to have my nose re-broken to straighten it out.

That brush with the bus meant I couldn't work and effectively ended our hopes of moving south. It also left us homeless and we had no choice but to go and stay with my mother as I had been told I would be unable to work for a long, long time. In fact, it was so bad that, at one point, I feared I'd never get back onstage again. During my recuperation, Shirley, the kids and I remained at my mother's and I was eventually put in touch with an agency called Chalmers Wood Ltd. It was run by a nice fella called Peter de Rance who was, and still is to this day, Andy Cameron's agent. Peter got me a booking for a summer season on *The Lex McLean Show*. I then did a couple of seasons in 1965 and 1966 in Rothesay with Larry Marshall at The Winter Gardens. Larry was a lovely person and a great guy to work with.

We rented a flat on the Isle of Bute with Ken Flowers who was a good piano player. We christened our accommodation The Gaff and to say it was brutal would be too kind. I was the resident cook and, every Friday night, I would make a beef stew with just about everything in it. We'd open some bottles of wine and most of the cast would come over and visit. Ken Flowers used to clean the place up – he was particularly good at washing the floor. But The Gaff was where everyone seemed to head to and we had many laughs of an evening.

The next year, when I returned to Rothesay again, I was on with the comedian Billy Rusk. Now comics are altogether a different breed. Long before I came along, it was always the comic who topped the bill and, in time-honoured tradition, Billy Rusk was top of the bill in Rothesay. Peter Devance had booked me to do a double act with a girl called Esther Hart. Esther was already one half of an established double act with her husband Mal Hollander and they toured as Hollander and Hart. They were a great act – one of the best I've ever seen. Mal did a bit of yodelling and guitar and Esther did a Chic-Murray-style routine. She had a very dry sense of humour and was great at pulling all the faces – she really was very good. Although professionally they were very sound, their marriage was on the rocks and I presumed this was the reason I was to be forming a new double act with Esther. Unfortunately, that never really got off the ground as Esther got friendly with this guy in a group called The Freemen and the whole situation became a bit complicated and messy. However, I had signed my contract and I was going to be there for the season come what may.

I would open with the song 'Come In, Come In (It's Nice to See You)'. One night, just to be different, I sang it in the style of Andy Stewart, with a bit of a comic twist, when suddenly, halfway through the song, my microphone went dead and I was singing into nothing. I came offstage to see what had gone wrong and Billy Rusk was standing there with a face like fury. He shouted at me, 'I'm the f***ng comedian here – I do the gags!' And Billy wasn't finished there. When I went back on to do my own main spot, lo and behold, the bastard had switched my amplifier off so no one could hear me play the guitar.

This time, it was my turn to lose the head. I stormed to Billy's dressing room but he knew what was coming so he had locked the door. I was kicking and hammering on it so hard that I nearly took the door off its hinges. Eventually, Billy opened the door and I grabbed him by the collar and said, 'You ever do that again, ya bastard, and I'll kill you!' It just shows you what a tough, tough business this can be when you had to fight just to survive. That's the worst side of this profession. The game is hard enough, especially when you're starting out, without someone sabotaging your act. That's why, in later years, I went out of my way to at least try to give people a hand.

I have never fallen out with people that I've chosen to be part of my show. If you employ people, they are part of your team and they're there to take the pressure off you. The support acts have to be good so that they can get the crowd going and everyone in the audience is in a happy mood when the top of the bill comes on. You don't want the opening act to be crap but Billy Rusk did. People like him – and Billy Crotchet over in Germany – found it impossible to think beyond themselves. The good of the entire show was never uppermost in their minds. It was all about what they could take out of it and that side of things really saddens me. The incidents with both of them made me think what a terrible profession I was part of – and it really didn't have to be like that. I must have about ten thousand scars on my back from all the stabbings and that, unfortunately, is how the profession works.

However, that season in Rothesay wasn't all doom and gloom. At the time, my mother was going to Canada to see my brother Andy. Shirley brought her down to Prestwick Airport and I met up with them to see my mother off. After a lovely day, I decided we would spend the night at a bed and breakfast. We went to this place called Coral Mount in Queens Terrace in Prestwick and I thought it was very nice. Since we had no home of our own and The Gaff in Rothesay was nothing short of a hovel, I suggested that Shirley should just stay in the B&B for the entire summer. So Shirley cut a deal with the owner, Miss Turnbull – or 'that right old bitch' as she used to affectionately call her – for a cheaper rate.

There were no en-suite rooms in Coral Mount and Shirley was always getting a hard time from Miss Turnbull for washing nappies and using up all the hot water and nonsense like that – these old landladies were all heart. But then, one day, Miss Turnbull could have knocked Shirley down with a feather when she said, 'Mrs Shirley (which was what she always called her), do you want to buy this place?' As it had three floors, with ten rooms and a terrace, Shirley said, 'We could never afford a place like this.'

To cut a long story short, although it was something we could ill afford, Shirley went to the bank manager at The National Commercial Bank – this was before it, like many other smaller banks, was taken over by the Royal Bank of Scotland – and pleaded her case with the manager John McMillan. She told him that we had four permanent residents who came with the property and their rent would be enough to pay the mortgage. Anything we managed to take in over and above that would be a bonus. Unlike today, when you can virtually walk into any bank on the high street and get a mortgage agreement on the spot, banks back then thought they were gods and they turned down more people than they accepted for mortgages. Anyway, Mr McMillan listened carefully to Shirley's case and then said, 'I believe in you, Shirley – I'll give you whatever you want.' It was virtually unheard of for a bank manager to say that but, then again, our Shirl is extremely persuasive. She had obviously made a great case and that's how we ended up in the hotel business for many years to come.

It was also the moment that the Devines became solvent. It was a huge turning point in our lives as Shirley made a massive success of the bed and breakfast and this allowed me to travel the length and breadth of the country doing gigs – or skiving about as Shirley would put it – without the added pressure of trying to pay all the bills. We could actually have lived off the income from the B&B alone.

Shirley cooked the guests breakfast, lunch and supper. She also did baby-sitting for guests, on top of looking after our own two – she was an absolute marvel. Some great people, from air traffic controllers and customs officers at Prestwick Airport to holidaymakers from the south of England, came to stay there and it really did become a flourishing business. I'll freely admit that the success of the B&B was all down to Shirley as I was hardly ever there – although I did come back long enough to get her pregnant with our third and last child, Scot.

With everything running so well on the home front, I decided to try the Yorkshire clubs again. It was a thriving scene down there but it required a lot of hard work to be successful. It was like having to learn a completely new side of the business. I suppose I've always been a survivor but working those clubs didn't half toughen me – and many others – up.

My first introduction to the clubs was at a place called Firth Park Working Men's Club in Sheffield. When I walked in, the concert secretary – concert secretaries were like gods in these places – said to me, 'Are you the turn?' Laden down with a guitar and amplifier, I stood there in my lounge suit and replied, 'Err, yes, I am.' 'Right, well,' he continued, 'we'll be needing six spots off you, lad.' I said, 'I've only got two spots.' To which this guy says, 'Well, you'll need to find another four. You go on and do a couple of songs and then we'll have four games of bingo. Then you do another couple of songs and then we'll have another four games of bingo and so on.' At that time, acts were only there as entertainment between the bingo sessions – bingo was king. But, once I had tested the water, I began to get a feel for what they wanted. The crowd liked good singing and big ballads so it was all 'My love is like a red, red rose' and the like but, as my confidence grew, I'd finish up with a wee bit of rock 'n' roll.

It was a school of hard knocks, believe me. I remember going into one of the clubs where, if they didn't like you, they gave you a show of hands. They'd just throw an arm up in the air and you'd know it was time to wrap up proceedings. Fortunately, that didn't happen to me too often but it certainly made performers try their best and acts quickly adapted to what the crowds wanted.

There were times when audiences weren't that keen on what I was doing but I was never 'paid up'. Paid up is when a performer is told, 'Don't bother with the second spot, sonny.' I've seen that happen loads of time. Once I was playing just outside Doncaster and this turn was late arriving. He'd come from London and found trying to get to this place on the buses almost impossible. He then rushed onstage and started doing Frank Sinatra songs – really badly. In the middle of his second or third song, the concert secretary, sitting in his little doocot, cut the singer's microphone and announced, 'Ladies and gentlemen, I'll have you know we'll not have any more of this bloody rubbish here tonight. Right, lad, off the stage.' As I said, they were tough places but, fortunately, that was one humiliation I never had to endure.

Although it was hard work, it could also be very enjoyable – especially if you'd won them over. I'd play what was called Noon and Night. This was a Sunday speciality and you'd play your first gig in the afternoon. The all-male audience would have been there since first thing in the morning and, if you were any good, the place would be mobbed at night as they'd all come back with their wives. The money was fairly good too – for a Noon And Night, you'd maybe get something like £15 for one day, which was not bad in those days.

While I was down there, I worked for two guys. One was Slim Farrell – his real name was Stan Farrell and he was called Slim because he weighed about thirty stone. Slim was a very fair man – one of the fairest agents I've met. He was always straight with his acts and gave them everything they were due. This was not the case with all agents. The unscrupulous ones would book a performer into a club and, although the club would be paying £50, the agent would tell them the fee was only £30 and they'd keep £20 for themselves. The really bad ones would also take a percentage of the turn's reduced cut so that the agent would end up with practically the same money as the performer.

Slim was never like that. If the fee from the club was £30, that's what he'd give me and then I'd pay him his commission. I was surprised he was so honest as he was a terrible gambler and loved the horses. He'd sit in the club with his own telly on, watching the racing, and he'd be betting as much as £300 a time. I worked the clubs on Slim's circuit for about two years and he would send me anywhere from Sheffield to Newcastle and the North East to work for a few weeks. Then I'd get a call from him and discover I'd be off to Wales next.

One time, Slim sent me to play a club in a place called Tredega, close to Aberfan in North Wales. I arrived as usual with my guitar and amplifier and was met by the secretary who said, 'Can I help you?' I explained that I was the entertainment for that night only to be cut off in mid sentence. 'Oh no, you're not,' he said before explaining that they had Gladys Morgan, a big Welsh superstar coming in. So I held up a piece of paper with my confirmation on it but the guy was most insistent. 'We phoned your agent, bhoyo, and cancelled,' he told me. At this point, a really elderly lady, who turned out to be the Welsh superstar they were expecting, arrived. She looked like a Welsh equivalent of Gracie Fields. Seemingly, they were paying this old dear something like £200 or £300 to do the usual number of spots but she had decided that she was only going to do one half-hour spot. Places like that pay for their entertainment turns to do four or five spots and I could hear the secretary frantically trying to persuade her to do longer. While this was all going on, I packed up my car, said cheerio – and good riddance – and got ready to drive off. Suddenly the club secretary came running out into the car park after me and said, 'You're on!' I looked over to see his headline act, this ageing Welsh superstar, getting into her car. The car sped off down the road and I learned that she wasn't going to go onstage so I knew they were in big trouble. I said, 'Wait a minute, a little while ago you told me to sling my hook and now, all of a sudden, I'm on? Get lost!' The secretary pleaded and pleaded with me so, in the end, I agreed to go on.

I was sharing a dressing room with Lennie Leighton. Lennie was a cracking comic and, tragically, he'd lost two children in Aberfan Disaster. He had actually been in the audience to see Gladys Morgan but they'd dragged him out of the crowd and persuaded him to do a turn too. I told Lennie what they had put me through – telling me to sling my hook before begging me to come back on – and he said, 'Tell them to double your money.' I was on £25 but he said I should ask for £50. Now, as I have said repeatedly, money isn't the motivator for me so I said to the club secretary, 'I'll give you one spot for nothing and, if the crowd likes me, it'll cost you £50.' He was so desperate he agreed to it without hesitating.

Lennie Leighton went on first and did his routine which was about this old dear doing a runner. Even though the crowd were disappointed because they weren't going to see the act they thought they were going to see, he had them eating out of his hand. When he'd finished, he then said, 'Now we've got a young lad who's driven all the way down from Scotland to be here tonight,' and he went on to tell them my whole story – how I'd been mucked around by the club secretary, the lot. He finished up by saying, 'Here's how it is – I haven't heard him but he's from Scotland so I think he'll be a good act as there's not many bad Scottish acts around. He's also an honest boy and says he'll do his first spot for nothing but, if you like him, he'll do two – so give a warm round of applause for Sydney Devine.'

I had never had an introduction like it and it probably remains the best introduction I've ever had. So I went up and, before I'd sung a note, the place went wild. I started off with a nice wee up-tempo song, 'They're Gonna Put Me in the Movies', and then I did a couple of big Tom Jones numbers – 'We'll Keep a Welcome in the Hillside' and 'The Green, Green Grass of Home'. Well, that was like shooting fish in a barrel in Wales. I finished up with 'Red, Red Rose' and the place just erupted. The club secretary walked up to me after my first spot, shoved £50 into my hand there and then and told me to give them another spot – it just shows how you can turn a disaster to your advantage.

Those clubs were great training and I undoubtedly became a much more rounded entertainer because of it but it was hard on the home life. If I was lucky, I would get home every second weekend, making the long slog north in my Renault Dauphin, which was the equivalent of a Fiat Panda. And all those miles I travelled were on roads that are nothing like the motorways we have these days.

The truth is that I simply wasn't there for the kids – Shirley brought them up. I might as well have been in the merchant navy or something. It was almost a case of,

'Mummy, who's that strange man coming in the door?' – 'That's your father, children.' Fortunately, she did a brilliant job all on her own but that was the price I had to pay for being part of this profession – there weren't too many gigs close to home.

It was a difficult scenario. It wasn't an ambition thing that kept me going – it was as if someone had programmed my brain to believe that performing was all I wanted to do. Being up there onstage was my only goal. I never thought of career structures or anything like that. My only need was to perform and it's hard to explain to people who don't have those same needs why I made all those sacrifices.

Then, ironically, even though I just said that there were rarely gigs close to home, I ended up with just that – I came back to Scotland and secured a weekend residency at a place called the Finlayson Arms in Coylton, a little hotel just outside Ayr. And the money was good – not brilliant but enough for me to start living as a family again.

The Finlayson Arms seated about 120 people and I really built the place up. After a while, you could not for the life of you get in there. A bus used to come from the neighbouring village Drongan and, once the Drongan bus party was in, you couldn't get through the door of the Finlayson Arms. I was on guitar, the drummer was Jimmy Meechan from Ayr and the piano player was Gordon Brownlie. Our trio played every Saturday and Sunday and people came from all over to see us. Folk still talk to me now about the days at the Finlayson Arms in Coylton. I don't know what it was about the place but the atmosphere was so friendly – it was really more like a big party. We'd do our set then get people from the audience to come and give us a song – and this was long before the days of karaoke. Some wouldn't sing but would tell a joke instead. We were always having a laugh. I remember spotting a woman going off to the ladies' toilet and I told the crowd that when she came out I'd stop the music and we'd all give her a huge round of applause. Of course, when she came out and everyone started clapping, her face turned beetroot. Then I asked her, 'Could you hear us in there?' She said, 'No – why?' and I replied, 'Cos we could hear you!' As I said, it was a real party atmosphere and I spent two years there in the late 1960s.

During that time, I had started doing some of the working men's clubs in Scotland. It was nothing like the thriving scene down south and, to be honest, after what I'd learned in places like Sheffield and Wales, playing the clubs in Scotland was a piece of cake. And I was able to make a crust – especially when a guy called Sam Young, who ran the M&M agency in Wishaw, booked me up for The Pulp and Papermill Club in Fort William. Sam was paying me £25 for the show but he had hit on the idea of selling my photos at the gig for a few bob a print. Well, we made more from those pictures than I did on the fee and that was my first introduction to how lucrative merchandising could be.

11

HOW TO MAKE MONEY
JUST LIKE THAT

A local businessman in Ayr called John Scarlet was a builder by trade and he bought the town's Darlington Hotel. I first started doing gigs for him in 1971 when it was still quite a small venue. I had told him that, if he made it a larger venue, he'd be able to attract bigger names and John decided to take my advice and expand it. After all the alterations, John hired me to be his booker as well as his compère and warm-up act. Between us, we made the Darlington the best venue in Ayr and some of the biggest names in showbiz appeared on our bill.

I managed to hire the likes of Vince Hill, Bob Monkhouse and Tommy Cooper for stints there – some were good, some great and sadly others, like Tommy, I felt, short-changed the audience. Tommy was a £1,000 a night man so, for his six nights, he walked away with six grand in his pocket. But, every night before his show, we had to go out trawling the bars looking for him and he'd have us in a right sweat. He'd only ever be in a bar about five minutes away from the Darlington but, of course, when Tommy Cooper walked into a bar, the entire place wanted to buy him a drink. I don't think he bought a single drink for the entire time he was in Ayr. In all fairness to him, he did always make it onstage just in the nick of time but it didn't stop you being on tenterhooks until that huge frame of his filled the doorway.

Now, don't get me wrong, I liked Tommy and our boozing sessions after the show were quite phenomenal. To this day, I have never seen a man with the capacity to drink that Tommy had and, bear in mind, I'd toured with The White Heather Group. Quite simply, Tommy was a gold medal drinker. No one could shift the booze quite like Tommy. He could easily down a large brandy with a Carlsberg special, followed by a large whisky and a pint of Guinness – and that was just for starters. He could continue that way right through to the early hours of the morning, mixing spirits, beer, wine, you name it and none of it seemed to have much of an effect on him. I think everybody was intrigued with his capacity for drink and the fact that he was never up nor down with it. You certainly could never keep up with him. I never saw him drunk – or maybe it's more accurate to say that perhaps I just never saw him sober.

Besides his quite heroic drinking capabilities, Tommy was a very ordinary person. He was a massive man and, when he was standing next to my five-foot-seven-and-a-half-inch frame, he always seemed about twelve foot tall. I found him to be extremely jovial and the kind of person who wouldn't say or do any harm to anyone. I also think he genuinely considered himself very lucky to be in the position he was. Now I may be speaking out of turn here but I don't know if he ever enjoyed the business. What I mean is that I always think everybody in the entertainment business essentially loves what they do but I just don't think the same could be said of big Tommy. Sure, he enjoyed it to a certain extent but I think half the time – like when he'd make mistakes onstage and try to correct them with his little laugh and his catchphrase 'just like that' – his heart wasn't truly in it. He didn't seem to get the same buzz as the rest of us when trying to win over a new crowd. For most entertainers, it doesn't matter if that crowd you're playing to is made up of thirty or 3,000 people and nor does it matter if you're being paid a tenner or a thousand quid – you're there and you want to enjoy it and make sure the audience loves it too. But I don't think Tommy ever truly gave his best at the Darlington.

Maybe it was impossible for him to perform to the best of his ability when he drank as much as he did – I don't know. All I do know is that Tommy was a huge star when he came to play for us – one of the biggest names on TV at the time – and I was disappointed with him and I think the audience were disappointed too. When you'd see Tommy on TV, it was just for ten minutes or so and it was hysterical but, at the Darlington, he had to be onstage for an hour and, if I'm honest, it was sixty minutes of unstructured drivel. He seemed to just be going through the motions and, for that reason, I felt as though he cheated us slightly.

I don't think Tommy was the only big name who was guilty of doing that though – some stars play on their reputations. I remember, years after Tommy, I went to watch Pavarotti at the SECC in Glasgow and paid £78 each for two tickets for Shirley and me. He would come on, sing two songs and walk off. The orchestra would play on while he was offstage and then he would be back to do another couple of numbers. And that was the script for the entire night. In total, he must have sung for something like forty minutes out of a two-hour concert. I don't know what makes them do that to their fans – after all, it's the fans who have made them as famous as they are and, to me, not giving them their money's worth at live performances is disrespectful. The desire to do your best should always be there and, when it's not, it's time to throw in the towel.

I clocked up thirty-one years at The Pavilion in 2005 and I hope I've given people a certain standard every year. It's like running a restaurant – if you give someone a bad meal, that's the one they remember and that's the one that makes them have second thoughts about coming back again. Well, at the Darlington, Tommy served up six bad meals so, no matter what a lovely man he was, that's what I remember the most about him.

But, while Tommy may have failed to set the heather alight, it was a different story with Bob Monkhouse. Like Tommy, Bob was a lovely person offstage but he would also put on a truly excellent performance every single time. Right up until the moment he went onstage, Bob would sit in his dressing room, listening to the nine o'clock news to see if there was anything he could use from it in his act – now *that's* what I call topical. He also carried joke books with him everywhere he went and wrote all his gags down but I honestly don't know if he needed them as he seemed to have a photographic memory for gags and could reel them off, one after another, nonstop all night, if you let him.

Bob wasn't on as big a fee as Tommy was although we're still talking around £4,000 for seven nights – in the early 70s, that was a lot more than the average working man's annual wage. Bob also did an entirely different act for each night whereas, with Tommy, it was exactly the same, with just the slightest of variations when he mucked up. Bob was also extremely sharp and would shape most of his show around the audience. He'd ask someone, 'What's your name? Flora – oh, do you spread easily?' And that was him off, with the crowd eating out of the palm of his hand. Some of his stuff was really quite risqué for back then but he was a true genius and an ultimate professional. In fact, I used to tell every new comedian who worked with me that they should go and watch Bob Monkhouse and learn.

Sadly, I don't think he ever came across the same way on television. He always looked slimy and smarmy and I know a lot of people thought he was a real turn off but live onstage I don't think he could be bettered. If you speak to some of the best comedians around today, those worth their salt will tell you that Monkhouse was the king of comics. Before he started performing himself, both he and his partner Dennis Goodwin used to write scripts for other comics like Bob Hope – so, if he was good enough for Bob Hope, he was certainly good enough for us at the Darlington!

Tommy was a famous drinker and another who would fall into that category was Matt Munro who, at the time I met him, was a two-bottles-of-whisky-a-day man. Sinatra had said that Munro was one of the best British singers he'd ever heard – well, obviously Frank hadn't heard of me at that point! I booked Matt to appear at the Darlington for a week and we were completely sold out. He was a great entertainer with a beautiful voice and the crowd loved him. But, afterwards, he always had a right heavy session and it's quite something to watch someone being able to sink two bottles of whisky by themselves, every night.

One time at the Darlington, I had to tell one of our turns to put her knickers on – which was the first time I've ever told a girl to do that! The knickerless lass was Kathy Kirby who was this beautiful blonde bombshell who worked with a band called Ambrose's Orchestra. She was the band's lead singer and she had had a big hit in 1963 with a revamped version of the Doris Day song 'Secret Love'. She was still releasing top-ten albums when she played with us in the early 70s but, tragically, her life had started to go out of control – I believe some romance had gone sour and completely screwed up her mind. She was hitting the bevvy and the pills like nobody's business but she was still quite a performer. However, on this particular night, she was probably going to put on a show that no one in the audience expected.

Kathy was getting ready to go onstage when the lights at the side lit up her flimsy dress and it became obvious that she wasn't wearing any knickers. Now, I was the booker and the compère so it was my job to tell her. I said, 'Kathy, you can't go onstage like that.' She replied, 'Oh, can you tell I'm wearing nothing?' And I shouted, 'Yes – go and find your knickers!' which she promptly did. I really liked Kathy and so did the crowd. She was such a nice person and I hated to see how things were going wrong for her. It's sad to see that happen to any artist or anyone with God-given talent – such as a footballer who hits skid row. It's such a total waste.

I once managed to book Jimmy Tarbuck and the singer Kenny Lynch who had a big hit with 'Up On The Roof'. They were to perform at the Darlington at a time when the Open Golf tournament was being held at Troon. One night, Gay Brewer, an absolute golfing legend with the most unorthodox swing, had come to see the show and he asked me if I could organise a good table for the Friday night. He was with another golfer, Lanny Wadkins, and they were sharing a room at the Marine Hotel in Troon. But Gay warned me that, on Friday, he would be bringing a very special guest along although he wouldn't tell me who it was. He wanted it to be a big secret. That Friday was the second night of the Open and the place was heaving but I was desperate to see who Gay was bringing with him. So I couldn't believe it when I came offstage and, in my dressing room, Gay said, 'Hi, Sydney, I'd like you to meet my special guest – Glen Campbell!' Glen was over to see the golf because he was a big pal of Lanny Wadkins and he was actually sleeping on a bed settee in Lanny and Gay's room as you couldn't get accommodation for love nor money when the Open was on.

Before this, Glen had never even been to the UK, never mind Scotland, so this was his first taste of a British crowd. He was also one of the biggest stars on the planet at that moment and, in the week he turned up at the Darlington, he had no fewer than three songs in the top ten including 'Honey, Come Back', 'Wichita Lineman' and 'All I Have to Do Is Dream'. I was compèring before Tarbuck came on and, after him, it was to be Kenny Lynch's slot and then my solo stint. Before the dancing started, I did the usual thank yous to the crowd and I also said thanks to Gay Brewer and Lanny Wadkins. Then I added, 'And, by the way, there's also a gentleman at Mr Wadkins table – a real-life superstar from America who, at this very minute, has three songs in the top ten. Please put your hands together for Mr Glen Campbell!' Then this very handsome guy, with blond hair and that familiar all-American-boy look, stood up and I think the crowd just couldn't believe it. At first, they were dumbstruck and then they all started cheering and went totally wild.

I walked back to my guitar stand, picked up my guitar and just held it up. Glen took my cue and marched right up on to the stage, took my guitar and turned to Jimmy Cosker, who was the resident musical director, and asked, 'What have you got in the book?' Well Jimmy just was totally lost for words. Jimmy was trying to compose himself and Glen asked him, 'What do you want to play?' Eventually, Jimmy managed to splutter out, 'Er, whatever you want.'

He started off with a jazz number called 'Lover' and then went on to Sinatra's 'Strangers in the Night'. He didn't particularly want to sing. He had started his career as a session guitarist and all he really wanted to do was play. But, eventually, he took to the mike and sang 'By the Time I Get to Phoenix' and the whole audience was on their feet. The crowd had paid to get Tarbuck, Lynch and Sydney Devine and ended up with forty minutes of Glen Campbell for nothing and all because I'd been nice to Gay Brewer!

Afterwards, I said to the owner John Scarlet that Glen Campbell was in his hotel and he turned round and said, 'Oh really? What's his handicap?' He thought he was a golfer.

But it was one of those special nights that people talk about for years. I would meet Glen on three other occasions after that and he always remembered that night in the Darlington. I think it stuck with him because he was such a big star at that point but, here in Scotland, he was allowed to go back to his roots, let his hair down and have a blast. It was one of the best moments of my career.

My stint at the Darlington lasted about nine months and I enjoyed every minute of it. The only problem with the place was it had this lovely big room to perform in but there were simply not enough big names to fill it. The likes of Cooper and Monkhouse were really one-offs and, after they'd appeared, folk were looking for the same standard again. I did manage a few other coups including landing Tony Christie who was simply sensational onstage and not a bad golfer too. I played three rounds with him over the course of the week and he was a nice ordinary person. He had a lovely voice but was also a great worker. He was a huge name at the time and couldn't have been nicer to the fans. I usually find that the huge stars, like Christie and Campbell, are always the business – it's the in-betweens or those trying to make it who really are the pits. That's why I was so delighted at the start of 2005 when Tony Christie, along with the comedian Peter Kay, went to number one with Tony's old hit '(Is This the Way to) Amarillo' for Comic Relief and had a number one album. It just proves that, if you have real talent like he has, it never goes away.

I was pleased with what I had done for the Darlington and the star names I'd brought to Ayrshire. As well as Christie, Monkhouse, Tarbuck, Lynch, Munro, Kirby, Cooper and Vince Hill, I managed to bring Lonnie Donegan and Lena Martell to the Darlington. Lena had an unbelievable voice and it always surprised me she was never a bigger star than she was. You would be hard pushed to put on shows with the same calibre as those acts nowadays. It was a special era and I was just fortunate I got to work with all of them.

John Scarlet was also a great proprietor and money was no object for him. I remember once, when Scotland were playing England at Wembley, John had arranged to take all his friends and family down to London for the weekend. At that time, our third and last child, Scot, was only a baby so I said we couldn't go. Scot had been born on June the 16th 1972 at Irvine Central Hospital in Ayrshire. At the time, we still had the guest house and Shirley was working full time until just before Scot was born – she's still a bit of a workaholic to this day.

Anyway, John was most insistent that we go to London and, when I said we were having trouble finding someone to look after the baby, he phoned up Shirley to try to persuade her. She told him the same story that we couldn't get anyone for Scot and John replied, 'Shirley, the Lord God made the world in six days – I'm only asking you to get a baby-sitter for two!' So we found a baby-sitter and went off to London.

Mungo King, a really nice local newspaper reporter with the *Kilmarnock Standard*, came with us too to record our trip on camera for his paper. On the Saturday morning, before the game, we all headed into the West End and went to a bar on Leicester Square where we started getting full of it before heading to Wembley. It was only when we were in the taxi on our way to the stadium that Mungo realised he'd left his expensive camera in the bar and we had to order the cabbie to do a U-turn and take us back. I rushed into the bar with Mungo and my brother George and asked the barman if he'd seen the camera. He said he hadn't but you could just tell that the guy was lying so George decided to have a word.

Now, George, who sadly is deceased, was the most incredible character. Everyone knew Geordie Devine and I swear that, at the time, he was probably better known in Scotland than I was. In his younger days, he was in the medical corps in the army and became the featherweight champion boxing novice while serving out in the Middle East so it was fair to say he was very good with his hands. George said to the barman, 'You've got exactly thirty seconds to produce the camera or you won't have a bottle left in this gantry. Sure, you can phone the police but that's not going to bother me because, by the time they get here, this place will be totally wrecked!' The barman thought for a second before reaching under the counter and producing Mungo's camera. I think he took one look into my brother's eyes and realised George was deadly serious. Scotland were beaten 1–0 on May the 19th 1973 but at least we could celebrate getting Mungo's camera back.

George had been invited to London as he had been friendly with John Scarlet ever since the time he was in the Darlington one night and he sorted out this guy who was creating a bit of a scene and getting out of order. John had asked Geordie if he could help him out and my brother said, 'Aye, sure, no problem.' George eventually got this big guy out to his car, which was a hard job as he was fighting and kicking out all the way there. George pushed him down into the seat and slammed the door shut but this idiot wanted to get out and fight some more. As he threw the door open, George just planted the most precise right hook to the guy's chin and knocked him out cold – I've never seen anything like it. The punch must have only travelled around six inches, right, but it was a straight KO. That was my brother George and, of course, ever since then, John was always in his debt.

Despite the result of the game, we had a fantastic weekend in London together and we didn't half shift some amount of drink. John had booked us all into Churchill's nightclub where he had also organised a huge reception for after the match. Sometimes, when you start drinking, you can never get enough and this was one of those occasions. After we left the nightclub, we went back in the hotel. We were still thirsty but, to our dismay, we found the hotel bar was shut. Scarlet was a Johnny Walker Black Label man and he asked the night porter to get him a couple of bottles. It was around three in the morning at this point so it shouldn't have been a great surprise when the night porter refused. It was a bad move on his part – you don't want to upset a crowd of Scotsmen looking for their whisky. So Scarlet ordered him to go and get the manager who duly turned up. John explained that he too was in the hotel game and this was no way to run a business and added, 'It's not as if we're being out of order – we just need two bottles of Johnny Walker Black Label on this table now.' But the manager refused to serve us as well, which was ridiculous as John was paying a fortune for us all to stay in that hotel. So Scarlet asked this fella what his title was and he said, 'I'm the night manager, sir.' John replied, 'Well, if you still want to be the night manager here by the morning, you'd better get me two bottles of whisky.' And that seemed to do the trick – we ended up staying up all night and having whisky with our porridge in the morning. That was John – he was a wealthy, generous man who liked to spread it about.

In 1974, we also went to the World Cup in Germany with John Scarlet. We were staying in a place called Rudesheim, a town on the Rhein just outside Frankfurt. We got on a supporters' bus to take us into Frankfurt for the Brazil game and I have never seen a bus park like it. There must have been something like a thousand coaches there that day. We pulled into our space and, lo and behold, who got off the bus next to us but my brother Geordie. He had decided at the last minute to catch a flight from Prestwick to Frankfurt and just jumped on the first bus that was available. He asked where we were staying and said he'd catch up with us after the game as we were sitting in different parts of the stadium.

I thought that would be the last time I'd see him beacuse there were so many people and it had been pure fluke we'd met in the first place. So, long after the match, which had been a no scoring draw, at about three o'clock in the morning, I heard this voice singing. Shirley woke up and said, 'I think that's your George.' I told her, 'Don't be so stupid, we're in Rudesheim, he's in Frankfurt and probably, by this time, he's on the plane home.' But no, as usual, Shirley was right – it *was* our George. He found us despite not knowing which hotel we were staying in or speaking any German – but that was my brother through and through. We got up, had a few drinks and, in the morning, we all headed off to the airport together.

George had brought a pal, Tam Guthrie, with him. Tam owned the Mercat Hotel in Cumnock. During all their partying, Tam had lost his passport but, because there were so many Scotland fans at the airport, they only checked our tickets and we were basically all herded back on to the flights. Before we arrived at Prestwick Airport, Tam and George were having a few drams and Tam said, 'Now, if they ask, you can vouch for who I am. Just tell them that someone stole my passport in Germany.' George said, 'No problem, Tam – of course I'll vouch for you.' At Prestwick, Tam got stopped at passport control and he had to explain how someone stole his passport in Germany. He then pointed to my brother and said, 'This is my pal, Geordie Devine, who will vouch for me.' Geordie replied, 'I've never seen that man before in my life!' and walked away. But that was our Geordie – always full of fun and the life and soul of the party.

Although my time at the Darlington had been great, I was about to discover that a tour I had done of South Africa in 1969 was about to change the course of my life forever . . .

12

THE SPRINGBOKS

I had once done a summer season with Andy Stewart in
Aberdeen. Andy was a great guy and a really big star – his
likes had never been seen before and will probably never
be seen again. He was briefly part of The White Heather
Group and recorded his famous song 'Donald Where's Yer
Troosers?' with us and I actually play guitar on it. We did it
for the Top Rank Record label for no royalties – just a
straight session fee. I got on very well with Andy and, on this
tour of South Africa during Christmastime 1969, there was
Andy, me, the Scottish fiddler Jock Morgan, the soprano
Sheila Paton, a piano player called Tony Osbourne and the
French illusionist and pickpocket, Dominique. Dominique's
act was phenomenal – he would have the watch off your
wrist without you feeling a thing.

The tour started in Johannesburg before going on to
Cape Town, Durban, Port Elizabeth and East London. Our
musical director was a guy called Bob Adams who came
from Hamilton. Bob was friendly with a man named Dan
Hill who worked at a record company called RPM Records
and he invited Dan along to have a look at me in the show
while we were in Johannesburg. Afterwards Dan said to me,
'You did quite a good job of those country songs. Do you
fancy making an album?' and of course I jumped at the
chance. He then asked me how many songs I knew and said
I'd need to record twenty-eight tracks. I claimed to know at

least twenty-eight country numbers – give or take a few lyrics – and, after the meeting, I immediately phoned Shirley and told her I desperately needed lyrics to a huge list of songs. So poor Shirley had to sit at the gramophone, trying to write down the lyrics for me! A few days later, we went into the studios and ended up doing something like twenty-four songs – enough for them to lay down two albums – in a day and a half and most of them were single takes. There was no music or anything to sing to – I just told them what key I wanted and off I went. They added the instruments later and that was that. I never thought any more about it and just got on with the tour.

At the end of the South African tour, we were each called in to the tour manager's office to get whatever money we were owed. During the tour, we had been paid a weekly wage but, if anyone needed extra money, they could ask for it and a record of these extra payments was kept so that the amounts could be deducted from what was due to be paid at the end of the tour. Fiddler Jock Morgan thought this was a great idea and he would get additions to his weekly pay all the time. He even used the extra money to fly his wife Rita out from London for the last two weeks of the tour and the pair of them stayed in the best hotels and they didn't hold back on eating and drinking either. Of course, when it came to Jock going to see the tour manager to settle up, he was in for a bit of a shock as there was very little of his cut left. However, he asked Jock how he would like this small amount paid – meaning whether he would like it in sterling or in rands. Jock enjoyed a drink and his reply was, 'Just pour it into a large f***ing glass!'

Jock was quite a character and, at Hogmanay on that same tour, the audience had bought the performers a gallon bottle of Scotch. At the bells, the bottle was handed to Andy Stewart but he still had the finale to do so he passed it to Jock. Quick as a flash, Jock looked at the bottle, looked back at Andy and said, 'That's no' much between one!'

It was quite an experience being in South Africa at the height of the apartheid era. Some of our roadies were Cape Coloureds, a name for people of mixed race who were shunned by both the whites and the blacks, and they weren't even allowed to walk into our hotels, never mind stay in them. At the same time as we were in South Africa, Engelbert Humperdinck, who had just had a huge hit with 'Release Me', was touring there too. Engelbert's South African promoter ordered him to stay out of the sun because Humperdinck took a really deep tan that made him look Indian and that would cause all sorts of problems. A dark-skinned Engelbert would not have been allowed in to certain places and white fans might not come to see him – incredible to think all of this went on not so long ago.

Despite the racial side, the South African gigs were great as we were playing to Scottish expats and Andy was a huge draw. I was doing a bit of country and rock 'n' roll and there was something like a fifteen-piece orchestra on the stage with us. They were fantastic shows and it was quite an experience.

A while after I'd returned home, the record label sent me a copy of the first record that I'd made in Johannesburg. It was called *Sydney Devine Sings Your Favourite Country Songs*. South Africa did not have a big record-buying public and sales of the album there weren't great so I didn't really think anything more of it. But, apparently, the South Africans took my record to a big conference in France, where record companies from around the world gather every year to do business, and RPM struck a deal with the Irish record label

Emerald Records for my album. Emerald then did a release deal with the distributors Decca.

In 1970, a year after I'd made the album, there was a record buyer for Woolworth's in Glasgow's Argyle Street, who was, ironically, called Miss Devine. She spotted my record because we shared the same name and decided to buy in a box of my LPs which was about twenty-eight records in total. The store then played my records over the tannoy and, lo and behold, they sold out on the first day. So Miss Devine ordered another ten boxes and they had completely gone by the weekend. That one girl in Woolie's, who just so happened to share my surname, started the ball rolling on my recording career – a career that would see me sell more than ten million records. The Lord does, indeed, work in mysterious ways.

I may have started selling records but I was hardly what you would call an overnight success. I still needed to make a livelihood so I continued doing the clubs in Scotland. But, as I began to sell more and more albums, slowly but surely I'd arrive in places like Tullibody and the venues would be busier and busier. I was still at the mercy of these clubs' house bands though. Some were good, a few were great and the others were just awful.

I knew the tide was turning, though, when they were charging on the door to see me – this was unheard of in working men's clubs. They didn't offer to pay me any more money, mind. I was still working for £15 a shot but now it was in front of around 200 paying customers so I decided to increase my fee. Around about this time, Radio Clyde had just begun broadcasting and they started playing my records too. There was a buzz and the press were suddenly writing about me. It was like a snowball – once it gathered momentum, it just kept getting bigger and bigger. It seemed like I didn't have a minute to myself. Every day I was getting calls asking me to go here or do that. It was hectic but I was loving it – I was so busy and I had basically moved to the top of the bill.

Emerald Records then approached me to do another album with the record producer Tommy Scott. Tommy had been part of a double act with his wee partner Jimmy Kelly and they called themselves the Scott Boys. They had worked with Andy Stewart but Tommy got a bit disillusioned with life as an entertainer so he went to London to try to find work as a record producer and songwriter. He soon got the nickname Tommy B-side Scott because he'd go around all these record companies, selling them B-sides but, in the process, he made a fortune. He was a smashing songwriter and he later penned 'Scotland Forever' for me.

After his spell as Tommy B-side, he started working with people like Van Morrison and it was Tommy who produced Van's 'Here Comes the Night'. One day he took a call from Mervyn Solomon at Emerald Records who asked him, 'Hey, Tommy, have you ever heard of a South African guy called Sydney Devine?' Mervyn thought I was from South Africa because he'd bought my albums from the folk at the Johannesburg record company. Tommy chuckled, 'I don't know a South African called Sydney Devine but I've heard of a Scottish one – surely there can't be two of them?'

A few days later, Tommy got in touch with me and arranged for me to come to London to record the album *Cryin' Time* (Emerald Gem 1111). The title and theme of the album were all Mervyn's idea as he reckoned there was a bit of a market for sad songs. We certainly gave him what he wanted – there were fourteen killed in the first verse! The album was all weepies like 'My Son Calls Another Man Daddy', 'Nobody's Child' and 'Gentle Mother'. It would undoubtedly become the record I was famous for and, even when I eventually went to Nashville, people would say, 'Hey, you're the guy who sings all these sad songs.' Of course, I then had to start performing all these heartbreakers at my gigs. One night, before we went onstage, Bob Faloon, one of my acoustic guitar players, told me that he had just lost his mother the previous week. I thought the poor bloke was going to burst into tears onstage, especially as we still had to perform a line like 'We'll no' see you no more, gentle Mother'. I said to him, 'Jesus Christ, Bob, I'm sorry, I didn't know you'd lost her.' A big grin then crept across his face and he replied, 'Aye, what a f***ing good card game that was!' The bastard got me that time!

After the huge success of *Cryin' Time*, I then did *Absolutely Devine* with Emerald. However, despite selling records by the shed-load, I was getting virtually nothing back in the way of royalties from Emerald Records and, as you can imagine, after a couple of years, I was getting well and truly sick of the situation. Even without being in the charts, I was selling millions of records. It was incredible. Emerald was a budget label and sold my LPs for 99p each. To this day, my album *Cryin' Time* is still selling well. That one LP has probably sold three million copies and I've had virtually nothing from it. You hear of rip-offs in the music industry and it seems to me that this is a classic example. Emerald would repackage and sell *Cryin' Time* to subsidiary companies and, once they were finished with it, they repackaged it and it would be sold it on again and again. It was impossible to keep track of it so I'm probably being conservative with my estimate that it sold three millions album – it could well be double that for all I know.

And do you know how much money I have actually seen from that album? Well, put it like this, I must have received under £500 and I'm not talking about £500 a year, I'm talking about under £500 in the entire thirty-five years since its release. People might wonder how on earth I could have agreed to a deal like that but I was obviously not the only artist to suffer over the years. The truth is, when you're young and stupid – or just plain stupid as it was in my case – and somebody offers you a recording deal, you never actually get down to the nitty-gritty of asking how much it is worth. I don't think I even read the contract with Emerald. I was just so happy that my records were in the shops and selling like hot cakes – it was only later that I realised I was making an awful lot of money for other people.

Despite all that, I am remarkably philosophical about it all, even if I say so myself, because, without the success of *Cryin' Time*, I wouldn't be where I am today. It gave me an incredible platform – but, at the time, I was angry.

Then I got another call from Tommy Scott. He said he knew how unhappy I was with Emerald and a guy down in London called Ken Maliphant was now the Managing Director of Phonogram Records. Unbelievably, Ken was from Kilmarnock and, what was more, he wanted to sign me.

Having been financially stung before, I asked Tommy if there would be any money in it this time and was told there would be – as long as I wasn't tied to Emerald. Of course, Emerald soon got wind of my talks with Phonogram and suddenly they were on the phone trying to put the wind up me. Mervyn said, 'Oh, Sydney, you don't want to sign for a major label. We're a nice, small family company and you'll regret leaving us for the rest of your life.' I said that that was all well and good but they had given me virtually no money and Phonogram were offering me £35,000 just for my signature. Suddenly, this nice, small family company offered to match that advance on the spot so they obviously knew the cash cow they were about to lose. That made me even angrier because, if they were able to offer that amount of money – bearing in mind this was 1973 – then they were obviously rolling in it – and no doubt a lot of it came from sales of my records. So I said goodbye to Emerald, signed with Phonogram and, sure enough, I received a cheque upfront for the full £35,000. That was the most money I had ever had in my hand. Suddenly, I knew I had just stepped up a gear and was now in a whole new league.

With that signing fee, I bought a big house in Ayr. I was desperate to christen it Phonogram House in homage to the faith they had in me but, after much persuasion from Shirley, we decided to call it Vantana instead. The house had five bedrooms and we felt as though we were in paradise. The first thing I did was have a swimming pool built – well, I was a rock star now!

There was over an acre of land and half of that was lawn. Well, I use the term loosely as there was more moss than grass and it was like walking on sponge. The whole lot was in desperate need of some TLC. Just as I was wondering whether I might do the work myself, I was introduced to the most amazing gentleman. John Robertson was originally a dairy farmer at Patna in Ayrshire. He had taken to doing gardening work in his retirement and he seemed like the perfect person to fix our ailing lawn.

John arranged to take a look at it and, afterwards, got a farmer friend to come with a plough and plough the grass up. A week later, the farmer came back and scarified it and then John sowed the new seed by hand. Watching him was fascinating – he was a true pro – and, within a few weeks, we had a lush green lawn that we could be proud of.

A couple of months later, I was cutting the grass – Shirley kept the house and the garden was my responsibility – using a big petrol-driven lawnmower. I took the grass box over to the compost heap to empty it. Just as I got to the compost heap, which was about fifty yards away, I heard a phut-phut-phut noise and, in dismay, I looked round to see the lawnmower heading straight for the swimming pool. I dropped the grass box and sprinted towards the pool but, by the time I got there, the mower was lying at the bottom of the pool. Now, I wouldn't recommend trying to pull a heavy-duty lawnmower out of a swimming pool to anyone – especially when the pool is in Scotland and the water hasn't been heated! The water was absolutely freezing and, by the time I'd managed to get the mower out of the pool, I didn't know if I was Sydney or Cindy! However, it gave Shirley and the kids a good laugh.

Now that the garden was presentable, we decided we would have our first barbeque at Vantana. We invited our friends, the Tannock family and the Curlett family, to come over one Sunday. The pool had been cleaned after the lawnmower incident, the food had been bought and all we needed was the weather to be kind to us. Unfortunately, that was not to be and, at twelve o'clock, just as I was setting up the barbeque, the heavens opened. You never saw anything like it – the rain from those black clouds came stotting down – but I wasn't going to be deterred. We had a stable at the top of the garden for my daughter's horse but, because it was 'summer', Karen's horse was out in its field. So we moved all the food and drink up to the stable and used one side of it as a bar and the other side was to be where I would do the cooking.

Anyone who has ever barbequed will know that a lot of smoke is produced. Now, when you're barbequing outside, it's not too bad because the smoke disperses in the air but, in the confined space of that stable, it was a different story – the word 'kippered' comes to mind. I heard a strange neighing sound and lifted my head to see 'Sparky' Graham Tannock leaning over the stable door. He took one look at me and started singing, 'There's nae luck aboot the hoose, there's nae luck at all . . .' but replacing the naes with horsey neighing sounds! They were happy days, right enough.

My first album with Phonogram was called *Doubly Devine*. It was recorded in London and Tommy, who brokered the whole deal, produced it. We had the launch party for the album after a gig at Glasgow's Apollo Theatre. I decided to hold it there because, not long before the launch party, my gig at The Apollo had sold out. Well, when I say *my* gig that isn't strictly true – it was Charlie Pride's gig. Charlie was a black American country singer who had a big hit at the time with 'Crystal Chandeliers'. He was booked to perform at The Apollo but they couldn't sell the tickets. So Charlie's London agent booked me as his supporting act to see if they could get some more bums on seats and the concert ended up selling out. It's probably the first and last time in history that the support act has outsold the headliner. Pride's agent called and said he couldn't believe it – tickets had only begun to sell when they added 'with special guest star Sydney Devine' to the posters. After I had salvaged Charlie Pride's gig, you'd think he would have thanked me. Not a bit of it. The ungrateful sod wouldn't even talk to me – not even a simple hello. After his show, he came offstage and somebody had his coat ready for him. He put the coat on, slipped into the lane at the side of The Apollo, jumped in a car and was off. Not only did he not thank me, he never even signed one autograph. Afterwards, The Apollo's manager, Jan Tomasik, said to me, 'Syd, you could sell this place out on your own' – so I decided to have a bash at it. I had just done the deal with Phonogram so I thought there would be nowhere better to have the album's launch than at The Apollo.

Phonogram agreed and even hired a plane from London to bring loads of journalists and music industry types up to cover the launch. They also painted *Doubly Devine* on the side of the jet. They really pushed the boat out – or should that be plane? – for me and there were huge posters of me hanging outside The Apollo. I had never seen anything like it. I don't remember much about the show as it seemed to pass in a whirl but I do remember the crowd – they were just incredible that night. We had the party in Merchants restaurant afterwards and there were hundreds of folk there.

Billy Connolly even turned up as we shared the same manager at the time. He was as funny and outrageous as ever. Billy and I were quite friendly at that time – he's one of the few people in the entertainment business to have visited my house – but, that night, he was pretty smashed. I don't know if many people noticed the state Billy was in as we were all in full party mode. I was on cloud nine and I really couldn't believe this was all happening to me. A sell-out gig, a major record deal, the launch of my album, a jet with the name of my album painted on the side of it – it all seemed too good to be true.

The album would eventually go to number fourteen in the national charts and it made number one in Scotland. The whole thing was like a magical dream – especially because, just about a month before my big night, I had ended up in Heathfield Hospital in Ayr for ten days.

I had started getting incredibly sore heads and I couldn't get rid of them. They were so painful that I ended up banging my head against a wall – it was really that bad. When they took me into Heathfield, the pain actually got worse because they had to stop all my pain-control medicines so that they could see how bad it really was. They then took me up to the Glasgow's Southern General for a brain scan. That came back clear so they tried various pills and some worked but others were so strong they made my face go numb. My mother came down to visit one day and I'd been pumped up with so many tablets I couldn't speak. I was just a drooling wreck and she thought I'd had a stroke.

Anyway, after a whole battery of tests, they decided it was all just tension headaches, brought on by the imminent launch of my album and everything else I was doing. Ronnie Murdoch was the doctor who looked after me. His parting words to me were, 'Mr Devine, just go out and enjoy your success.' So I decided to follow the doctor's orders.

13

ANDY, WHERE'S YER TROOSERS?

I first worked with Andy Stewart when he took over the throne from Robert Wilson in The White Heather Group and we all instantly hit it off with him. This was after Robert's bad car accident which had left him feeling that working at the tempo he was used to doing was too much for him.

Andy worked with a guy called Dixie Ingram and, when they married two women who were sisters, they became connected through family as well as professionally. Andy married Sheila Newbigging and Dixie married Dorothy Newbigging. Dixie was a great Highland dancer and a lovely man – until he got in amongst the jungle juice, that is. The drink would totally transform him and he used to say some terrible things to Andy. We'd be driving along the motorway and one thing would lead to another and, before you knew it, the car would stop and they would get out on to the motorway verge and start fighting. They were always fighting. But it was quite funny because there was never a punch thrown between them – they would just scream at each other.

The second time I went to Australia on tour was with Andy. We played these massive rugby league clubs. They were brilliant venues, with ten-piece bands and packed to the gunnels with all the Scots who had come to see Andy. These clubs made their money on the one-arm bandits.

There would be a big entertainment hall that could sit 500 to 600 people and, downstairs, there would be another hall that had the same number of slot machines in it – it was quite an operation. Andy was some entertainer, the best Scotland's ever seen without a doubt and he revelled in this type of venue where he was backed up by a big band. He was doing all his impersonations – Dean Martin, Jerry Lewis, Satchmo, Gene Vincent, Elvis Presley – and he knocked them dead. He still had to do the Scottish songs with the hills and the heather but, between the songs, his impressions were something else. When he was in full flight, he simply couldn't be bettered. I had great respect for him and I'm so glad I got to see him perform in what was arguably his prime.

We were staying together in an apartment in Sydney with Ron Dale, who was a multi-instrumentalist. The three of us had a deal that we'd all do certain chores. So I would do all the cooking, Andy was going to do the cleaning and Ron's job was to do the laundry. Ron got the best deal, I reckon, as, obviously, you don't have to do the laundry every day. But I'd be slogging over the cooker, making three meals a day, while Ron lazed around in the sunshine. Eventually, Ron left for home and then it was just me and Andy left. By this point, we'd been away for so long that Andy was getting quite morose and depressed. We'd been away for two months and he was desperately missing Sheila, his wife. The funny thing was I never really took to Sheila. She was very prim and proper and she always called him Andrew. I was his supporting act and she treated me that way. I never enjoyed speaking to her. She had the uncanny knack of always making you feel like the pauper but Andy was the complete opposite and was very down to earth.

One night in Sydney, Andy had been particularly down when he suddenly announced, 'Right, I'm going up to The Cross.' By this, he meant he was going to King's Cross, the place in Sydney where all the prostitutes plied their trade. We had skelped a bottle of whisky between us when he decided he was going looking for a bit of fluff and he asked me if I was going to go with him. I said I wasn't but added, 'Let me tell you something, Andy. If you do go up to The Cross, be careful what you're doing as you're pretty well known.' So Andy decided to disguise himself by wearing a hat. I then told him to be sure to check the women didn't have big hands and Adam's apples because not all the dames up at The Cross were really dames.

I was in bed when Andy stotted in at about one in the morning and I asked how it went. He said that I had put him off – all the time he was there, he kept remembering what I'd said to him. 'In fact,' he said, 'there were some cracking-looking dames but I kept thinking about what you said about the Adam's apples and that worried me.' So, instead, he bought himself a Dunhill lighter and a box of cigars – that was his compensation present to himself for being good!

I loved my time with Andy and we became very close – just like brothers. As a person, he was kind and never interfered with your work – even when he was employing you in his shows – he just let you get on with the job. We got on like a house on fire then something very strange happened. In later years, when I was out on my own and starting to top the bill, we began to drift apart. I was doing bigger and bigger shows away from Andy and I knew he had been to see me about three or four times but he never popped in to say hello. I found that very strange as most pros will always nip backstage to check how you're doing.

Occasionally, Shirley would get a phone call from him when I was away working. Sometimes, when he'd had a wee drink, he'd be on the phone to her for about two hours so he ended up speaking more to her than to me. I did hear from him once or twice – he'd ring trying to sell me a car but I reckoned it was likely that he was trying to get rid of his own car. And that was it. It saddened me that our friendship ended up like that. I don't know if he resented me having success. I've thought about this long and hard and I would hate to think that was the reason. He never struck me as that kind of guy but, for the life of me, I can't think of any other reason. If it was a case of him resenting my success, then I don't think he should have begrudged me it – he knew I'd served my time with The White Heather Group and his show. I don't know how many years I worked before I finally got a break but it was a lot longer than Andy had done before success came his way. I had slogged around with Andy on and off for ten years so I always thought he'd have been delighted for me and would have told me so.

I'd had so many brilliant times with the man that I couldn't understand why he was behaving like this. One time, we did The Empire in Inverness for a summer season, along with Tommy Scott. I remember I got these digs at 5 Huntley Place where Rita Adams was the landlady and I think I ended up sharing her one letting room with dancer/producer Desmond Caroll and the fiddle player Angus Fitchett. The food was terrible and, one day, Angus said he thought we were all going to end up suffering from malnutrition through living there. Andy, being top of the bill, was staying in a fancy big hotel but he'd get so lonely that he'd come over and bunk with us in our hovel, just so he could join in with the craic. That was the kind of guy he was – although he was top of the bill, he was one of the boys. That's why, when he became so standoffish with me, it was hard to take.

Ironically, in later years, we ended up working for the same record company, Scot Disc in Glasgow. I would hear from the staff in there that Andy had sent his regards and such like but I would just never hear it from Andy himself. Of course, he was very, very ill latterly. He was on strong drugs to try to keep him alive and I heard through the grapevine he was having a lot of health problems, some of which people reckoned he was almost wishing on to himself. He wasn't exactly a hypochondriac but he was always insisting that he needed an operation for something that perhaps didn't really require surgery – as I said, he was very ill.

But, despite the deterioration in our relationship, I will always have my own fond memories of the man who was simply Scotland's greatest entertainer and a man who had one of the sharpest brains and quickest wits in showbiz.

Sydney's dad, Daniel Devine

A young Sydney who already looks
like he feels at home performing

Sydney, with his first guitar,
serenading his mother who was
known affectionately as Old Nellie

Sydney, wearing a kilt and with his
customised guitar, prepares to take
to the stage

Sydney, the rocker – but check
out those tartan trews!

Sydney and Shirley at the Gaiety
Theatre in Ayr, 1960

Sydney and Shirley's wedding, November the 11th 1961

Sydney with The White Heather Group, 1962

Fans flock to Glasgow's Pavilion Theatre to see Sydney, 1974

Sydney with the guys from Chappells Music – on the left is producer
Tommy Scott, next to him is Jimmy Henney, Chappells promotions man,
and on the right is Roland Rennie, the man who also signed Eric Clapton,
David Bowie, Status Quo and David Essex

Sydney meets the Queen at the Royal Command Performance during the
Queen's Silver Jubilee celebrations in 1977. Also in the photo are Ronnie
Corbett, Frankie Howerd, Shari Lewis with her puppet Lamb Chop, David
Soul, Dolly Parton, Lena Zavaroni and Allan Stewart

Sydney is the first UK artiste to be awarded a Gold Cassette.
Sydney got the award for sales of *Absolutely Devine* and doing
the honours in 1975 is Scotland Manager Willie Ormond

Sydney and Shirley, with their good friends Tommy and Mary Scott, enjoy a
trip in a Venetian gondola, Easter 1976

Cheers! The Devines in festive spirits. On the left is elder son Gary, then comes younger son Scot and seated between her mum and dad is daughter Karen

Sydney celebrates thirty years in showbiz with an engraved decanter presented to him by one of his loyal fans

Sydney playing Buttons in panto at the Gaiety Theatre, Ayr, 1987

Sydney poses for a publicity shot in his favourite Stetson hat, 1993

Sydney and Shirley with two of his most loyal fans, Liz and Harry Stevenson, at the celebration of the Stevenson's ruby wedding in 2001

Sydney and Shirley attending their son Scot's graduation ceremony at Robert Gordon's University in Aberdeen, 1998

Sydney cuts the ribbon at one of the twenty-plus Marie Curie shops
he has opened

Sydney and Shirley's six grandsons: (back row) Greg, Ryan and Ben;
(front row) Calum, Adam and Ali

jumped at the chance. Johnny McCallum, who's still there, was the driving force behind it. He's a real diamond and, for the first few weeks, he used to operate the decks for me and all I did was read out the requests. Then Tom Ferrie at Clyde said, 'Look, Syd, you'll find the show will be a lot tighter and much better if you learn to operate the decks yourself.' So Tom came in and showed me how to cue up the records. After that, I was a regular fixture on Clyde every Saturday morning and Sunday night for the next ten years.

Career-wise, things really couldn't have been going better for me and, after the success of my album *Doubly Devine*, it was back to London to record the follow-up, *Devine Time* – there's only so many puns you can get out of Devine. The album title was perfect as it was also the name of my STV show. The studio where we made the record was called Chappells Music. It was in Bond Street and is now PR guru Max Clifford's office. The first day we had a helluva session and did sixteen songs on the trot. We were all glad to get out of there and we went across the street to a little pub called The Grosvenor Arms to let off some steam.

There, we bumped into a little guy called Tony Peters who was a radio plugger. Tony spotted me and Tommy Scott and said, 'Hiya, guys, remember all the airplay I got you for *Doubly Devine*? How's about a drink?' The truth was that Tony had been no help at all in getting the record airtime so Tommy called him a liar and was about to knock his block off. The person who was actually responsible for the record reaching number fourteen in the national charts was Ed 'Stewpot' Stewart. Ed was on Radio 2 at that time and he championed my songs. It was really down to him that I managed to break into the national charts. I have to confess that there was a little bit of 'you scratch my back and

I'll scratch yours' though as Ed's father-in-law was Jimmy Henny who worked for Chappells Music where I recorded the album – but, hey, in this business you use whatever connections you can.

It was around about this time that I decided I needed my own band. So I called on the services of the following: George Payling, a bass player from Ayr; guitarist Ronnie Christie who is now living in Australia; Dougie Stevenson on steel guitar; drummer John O'Neil; and Bill Garden on piano. I called the band Ovation – I liked the sound of Sydney Devine and Ovation – but, after a year, I changed the name to Legend. They were a smashing band and, eventually, I had between 300 to 400 songs that we could play. All I had to do was tell them what I wanted to sing and, within seconds, they were on to it – amazing.

It was in the spring of 1974 that I played my first-ever gig at Glasgow's Pavilion – a theatre that was to become my spiritual home and still is to this day. It sold out almost immediately – which is something I'm thankfully still able to do thirty-one years later. So, because I sold out the first night, we booked the next night and that sold out, then the next and that went too. Before I knew it, I had sold out The Pavilion for a solid two-week stint. Prior to this, Lulu had been The Pavilion's box office record holder but now I have held that honour since those dates in 1974. Some of the same fans that were there thirty-one years ago are still in the audience now although, sadly, of course, some have passed on, the majority from those early audiences still come to see me.

I would say the only other venue that comes close to The Pavilion for me is the Theatre Royal in Norwich. Don't ask why – I simply don't know – but it always does well for me too. However, I have to say that, although I play to packed houses there, the atmosphere doesn't compare to that of The Pavilion. Glasgow people are unlike any other folk in the world. If they like you, they'll love you forever and, if they don't like you, they won't be slow in telling you. The thing is that you can't kid a Glasgow crowd on. They can spot a fake from miles away and I think they have always appreciated that I gave them 100 percent – they could see that I threw myself wholeheatedly into my shows.

But selling out venues like The Pavilion puts a lot more responsibility on your shoulders. For starters, you can't have sore throats. There have been times, at the beginning of a six-night run, when I've been suffering from a rasping sore throat – so bad that I couldn't even talk to anyone. However, knowing I had no choice, I simply forced myself to get through to the end of the week. In this business, if you take even one night off, you're letting people down and that's not on. Someone may have organised baby-sitting, bought some new clothes, arranged to meet friends and then you call off for some reason. Sorry but I'm a firm believer that the show must go on. I think that, in over fifty years of being in entertainment, I've only had to cancel four shows – and that was down to major heart surgery!

I remember, towards the end of my first stint of shows at The Pavilion, there was a guy who came up to the theatre and told the stage doorkeeper Les Harvey – Alex's dad – that he wanted to see me personally. Les didn't fancy letting him in to see me as he said he looked a bit dodgy. He was a wee guy and he was carrying a Marks and Spencer's bag. But curiosity got the better of me and I told Les to send him up. So this wee bloke came into my dressing room and said, 'I've got a present for your wife.' And, from the plastic bag, he produced a pastel-coloured mink jacket. It was beautiful and obviously worth thousands. I asked where he got it from and he shuffled from foot to foot before saying, 'Er, a friend of mine was needing money.' I told him I didn't buy stolen goods but he insisted it hadn't been nicked. He was after £500 for it, even though it was clearly worth ten times that, so I told him to come back the next night after I had had time to think about it.

Lo and behold, when I got home that night after the concert, on the STV news there was a report that a £5,000 pastel-coloured mink jacket had been stolen from a store in Ayr and, if anyone was being offered it, they were to call the police. What was even more frightening was that Shirley often shopped in this particular boutique. Can you imagine what would have happened if I'd bought her the mink and she had wandered into the place it'd been stolen from wearing it?

On another occasion, Les came up to my dressing room again and told me there were two official looking types at the stage door waiting to see me. Wee Les was very streetwise and always tipped performers off that way. It turned out they were warrant officers and had come to arrest the wages of one of the cast. I had no idea who these two warrant officers wanted but, quick as a flash, I told them, 'Sorry, you're too late. You should have come yesterday as I always pay my staff on a Thursday so that they can cash the cheque in time for the weekend.' Of course, it was a little white lie but that unnamed cast member was most grateful for it.

I always had great comedians in the show. In fact, I gave Andy Cameron his first theatre gig. In later years, Andy would refer to me in his act with gags like, 'If Sydney Devine can sing, then Crippen was innocent!' Comedians will do anything to get a laugh and, if that was what he needed to get the crowd on his side, then so be it – that's his job. In 1994, I remember doing a pro-am golf tournament down at Troon and Andy was having his usual dig at me. However, in the clubhouse afterwards, he did acknowledge the start I'd given him. He said, 'You know, Sydney was the first to employ me in the theatre twenty years ago' and I retorted, 'Aye, Andy, and you're still telling the exact same gags.'

Also, during that first stint at The Pavilion, a street vendor suddenly appeared outside selling Sydney Devine scarves with a photo of me on them. My guitarist, Dougie Stevenson, went up to the guy and said, 'You're not allowed to do this.' The bloke protested that everybody's allowed to make a livelihood but Dougie explained that the photo he was using was copyrighted as it was from one of my album covers. Dougie then established that the chancer was charging £1 a time but that the scarves only cost him 25p to make. So he cut a deal with this Glaswegian entrepreneur to bring a 1,000 scarves to the theatre the following night. We bought the whole lot from him for 50p apiece and sold them for a quid each – a nice little earner all round.

15

THE TRUTH ABOUT MY MARRIAGE

With my increasing popularity, the fans were growing in vast numbers. To tell you the truth, it was amazing and overwhelming. I was once doing a record launch in Woolworth's and the crowd was so huge they blocked the road. The police had to be brought in for crowd control as it was all getting a bit too wild, with so many girls just desperate to touch me. But, once they've touched you, the next stage is to rip the jacket off you. I had my jacket ripped off my back many a time and, when you're in the middle of a throng of hysterical women, jostling you around and ripping your clothes off, it's actually quite scary. Some wanted more than just my jacket of course and I had quite a few indecent offers – some of which I even refused!

Now, any man who thinks his wife is stupid is in for trouble and I knew, from very early on, that Shirley was as sharp as a tack. Any woman worth her salt would know that, if her husband was being pursued by thousands of female fans, then things might happen – it's inevitable. I think the thing to remember was that the most important person in my life was Shirley and I made that pretty clear to her right from the word go.

We didn't have any arrangement that said I could go and screw the world because no woman would put up with that

– women have a deep sense of pride. Maybe Shirley did suspect that I was still behaving in the same way as I had been when I was single but here we are still married to each other after forty-odd years. There was never, ever, ever, ever, anything would come between Shirley and me. So the subject of other women was something we didn't speak about. Shirley always knew I was coming back. So she knew and she made it very, very plain to me that she wasn't happy about it but it happened and we moved on.

Don't get me wrong, it did put our marriage to the test but marriages are put to the test all the time. Sometimes, marriages are under great strain because of financial pressure. Fortunately, we never had that to worry about since Shirley made such a success of the B&B and then my deal with Phonogram Records came along. Since then, Shirley has never wanted for anything in her life. She worked hard to keep us afloat in the early years and she raised the children more or less single-handedly but our life has been very comfortable for a long time now.

To me, marriage is like buying a house – it's full of compromises. When you're looking for a house, you are maybe hoping to find one you like in the country, with four bedrooms, two bathrooms and a nice garden. But you very rarely get all those things so you have to say, 'Well, I'll compromise on this or that.' I think marriage is a compromise as well and you should also be attuned to the other person's feelings. If you can do all that, then I think any marriage will stand the test of time and I highly recommend it.

But there's no denying it was difficult. I would go from being a family man at home to turning up for gigs where knickers galore were raining down on me. It was hard to switch off and go back to being just Sydney, the husband

and father, back at home. I'd go from having girls screaming at me to dealing with things in the real world, like reading my children's school report cards. It takes you a while to come down from the high of performing – there's no doubt about it.

When I finished at The Pavilion on a Saturday night, I'd get home and sit to maybe four in the morning to try to get myself back to reality. But that high is probably why people perform. The sound of applause, the adoration – they're every bit as addictive as a drug. In years to come, though, I managed to treat the gigs more and more as my working environment. It was my job. I was a rock 'n' roll singer or country and western star but, at home, I was just plain Sydney once again.

There have, of course, been times when I was tempted to sample the grass on the other side of the fence and it's fair to say that there were occasions when my standards fell short of what those of an ideal husband should be. I'll say no more on the subject except to quote the words of an old country song:

> I've never gone to bed with an ugly woman,
> But I've sure woken up with a few.

16

THE BIG O

I only ever had two managers in my life. One of them, sadly, from my point of view, was Henry Spurway who I got in tow with while I was still recording for Emerald. If there had been any justice in this world, when he had his first bath after he was born, the midwife should have kept the water and thrown Henry out instead.

When I first met Henry, he had a pub in Bellsquarry near Livingston. One night in 1974, after a few drams, he got me to sign a piece of paper. I honestly didn't know what I was signing but, as far as I recall, it wasn't a legal document. It just looked like a sheet of paper, the size of a news reporter's notepad – about four inches by four inches – but, in October of 1982, that small sheet of paper would cost me £40,000 at the Court of Session in Edinburgh. Henry said he was going to tell the Inland Revenue that I had been diddling them because he had paid me in cash for the gigs he had arranged for me and I hadn't been declaring this income. He said this was how I had been able to buy my wife fur coats and rings.

At the end, I would have done anything to get rid of him. *The Stage* newspaper had Henry on their banned list and advised performers not to sign a contract with him until they had been in touch with Equity, the union for stage professionals. The worst thing I did in my life was meeting

Henry Spurway and the best thing was getting rid of him. Getting him out of my life was costly but it was worth it.

My next manager was Frank Lynch and the difference between him and Spurway was like night and day. He worked under the banner of Unicorn Leisure and he also managed Billy Connolly at the time. Billy Connolly, the singer known as Christian and I were Frank's three main acts. Then, during the mid 70s, he sold his Billy Connolly contract to the London promoter Harvey Goldsmith. He also flogged all the discos he owned and rumour had it that he left for America with suitcases of money during a customs strike so no one could check what he was carrying. I don't know if that was true or not, all I do know is I never saw my manager Frank again. But, unlike some unscrupulous agents, he had always treated me fairly and, after that, I took to managing my own affairs using the name Sydney Devine Entertainment's Ltd.

Just before Frank did his disappearing act, he offered me the support slot on a Roy Orbison tour. He was very upfront about it and said there was virtually no money in it but they would be paying my band and our expenses. However, Frank reckoned it was an ideal opportunity for me to do more work in England. Now, the whole reason I wanted to break into England wasn't driven by ego or anything like that – it was simple economics. England was a far bigger marketplace than Scotland and, even though I'd reached number fourteen in the national charts, it was mostly down to Scottish sales. You can really only tour Scotland twice a year maximum. Even if you are touring with a new album, you can't constantly keep going back to do the likes of Inverness, Aberdeen, Elgin, Dundee as people will get fed up looking at you. So, the driving force behind doing the poorly paid Orbison tour was that it might lead to the possibility of branching out in to new venues.

Touring with the great Roy Orbison was a pretty big deal at the time but we had our problems from the start. I was all fired up for his shows and thought I'd blow the crowd away for Roy coming on. But, after the first night, his manager decided my material was too similar to Roy's own stuff so a comedian from Manchester was brought in to split us up. What had started off as my forty-minute warm-up slot was almost cut in half and I was left with just twenty-two minutes. We did fourteen shows together and it took Roy until the last night to say anything to me. When he did, he mumbled something like, 'You're going to be all over this place when I come back.' Apart from that, he hadn't said a single word to me.

But my manager, Frank, had been right about it helping to break me into England because the first night I did with Roy was at The Theatre Royal in Norwich and, ever since, I've been able to go back there on my own and sell it out. I also did my own gigs in Bournemouth, Liverpool and Southport off the back of that Orbison tour. However, although I may have only been on single sentence terms with the Big O, he didn't half put on some show. The lights would go down and all you'd hear was the thump of the drums before this incredible voice would fill the theatre with 'Only the Lonely'. After that, he'd do another fifteen songs, all of which had been top-ten hits. I only wish I'd been able to get to know him better.

But that was just one of those things. I don't think it's enough just to be a big star – you've got to have something else. I remember meeting Perry Como in Edinburgh around about the same time and you couldn't have met a nicer person in your life. The bigger the star the nicer they are is what I've always found. The only exception to the rule was Orbison. Maybe he had other things going on in his life at the time but, to me, there was no warmth from the man.

On that tour with me was the roadie George Miller. George worked for Frank Lynch and he had a sort of Friar Tuck haircut, bald in the middle with hair around the sides, and this massive bush of a beard. He'd also been Billy Connolly's roadie and, in fact, Billy even mentioned him in his first book, calling him 'my faithful roadie, George'. Well, now I've mentioned George too! He was quite a character and a very handy man to have around. One night, we were staying at the Holiday Inn in London with Orbison's band. George went to check out in the morning, only to discover the phone bill for my room was something like £280. George shouted at me, 'Who the hell were you phoning?' I protested my innocence, saying I never used the phone in the hotel room. George wasn't the greatest diplomat in the world and he turned round and told the receptionist, 'Mr Devine will not be paying this f***ing bill!'

It turned out that Orbison's band had somehow managed to charge all their calls back home to the States to my room. But George made sure it was very quickly sorted out and told Orbison's band not to try to pull a stunt like that again or there'd be trouble. So you can see why Billy Connolly and I liked having George around.

The funny thing is, he was the skinniest man I've ever seen. Once, we were touring up in Tain, in the north of Scotland, and we'd had a fair old skelp of the firewater when George passed out on top of his bed. The rest of us stripped him bare and took some photos but I've seen more beef on a McDonald's burger – he was just a bag of bones. I saw him in 2001 for the first time in ages and he'd shaved his beard off – I didn't even recognise him and I'm sure Billy would have had the same problem.

I always liked travelling and having a laugh with the band. My lead guitarist, Owen Knox, tragically, had to leave the band when he lost a daughter through an asthma attack when she was in her teens. He and I used to bounce off each other really well and he would come back and play with us when he could. We were staying overnight in Norwich after a show and we couldn't get a drink because this old night porter, who happened to be from Edinburgh, refused to serve us. He should have realised that nothing gets between a musician and a drink. We found our way into the bar where the shutters didn't offer too much resistance – castle doors could be breached by a thirsty band – and helped ourselves until four in the morning.

The next morning was beautiful and sunny and we decided to drop the hood down on my Mercedes to take in some rays and get some fresh air as we were still slightly the worse for wear. Owen and I thought we looked the business, posing away in my Merc SLC 500. We were cruising into Manchester on the way back up the road when we got stuck in a contraflow system that lasted about five miles. All the while, the skies were getting darker and darker until, suddenly, the heavens opened up – I'm talking about a torrential downpour here. We needed to get a place off the road to stop and pull the hood up but couldn't because we were struck crawling along in this single lane of traffic. Within about four minutes, there was literally about two feet of water at our feet and Owen and I were sitting there like two drowned rats with the shades on. Suddenly, we didn't look so cool and there were guys passing us in other cars and giving us two fingers. We were miserable and they enjoyed every second of our soggy discomfort.

It just shows that anything can happen when you're on the road with a band.

17

A NASHVILLE ADVENTURE

Doubly Devine and *Devine Time* were released on Phonogram Records and the next album I recorded for the label was *Almost Persuaded*. After that, I felt it was about time that I had at least one album recorded in Nashville instead of a London studio and fortunately Phonogram agreed. So they fixed me up with a phenomenal producer Don Schroeder, who had a company called Papa Don Productions in Nashville and I went over to live there for nearly two months. Don put together an incredible band for me with Jerry Carrigan on drums, bass player Tommy Cogbill, the guitarist Johnny Christopher and another guitarist called Reggie Young. Now these guys were *the* Nashville sound. Almost every record that came out in Nashville in those days, including some of the early Elvis recordings when he was with RCA, had these same guys on it. So, basically, I was recording with Elvis's backing band. I was just awestruck.

I'd sit in the studio during a break and listen to them talking about some of the biggest names in the music industry as if it was nothing – for example, I'd hear one of them say, 'That bastard Jerry Lee did such and such.' These guys weren't showing off – they were top sessions players and they had played for Jerry Lee Lewis, Roy Orbison and, of course, The King.

I have to say that I've worked with some outstanding musicians over the years but this lot were out of this world.

The bass player, Tommy Cogbill, would lay down a track like 'Love Me Tender'. He'd play it really straight but then, when we were finished, the producer, Don, would give him a massive joint – I'm talking about a Bob Marley special – and Tommy would stick another bass line on top of the original one so it would just sound really amazing. I was smoking in those days but I never touched what these guys were on – although they actually thought I had my own stash.

One day, during a break, I was smoking a packet of unfiltered Players and all the guys were staring at me. Eventually one of them said, 'Hey, man, are you not going to pass that around?' I apologised and handed over the pack and told them to help themselves. So they all had one and were like, 'Hey, man, that's something else, that's really good stuff, man!' – they thought they were smoking joints. They, in turn, always offered me a puff on their joints and I admit that I was tempted but I also know the kind of person I am – the type who never does things by half measure. I'm very committed in everything I take on. If I go out to do the garden, I have to do the whole lot in one day – rain or shine. And I knew, if I started with drugs, it would be the same – that's why they've always frightened me. I thought that, if I tried them once, I'd like them so much I wouldn't be able to stop.

I may have been just another pay cheque to these guys, but they never treated me that way and I loved the experience of working with them. Don Schroeder may have technically been in charge but every one of these musicians were producers in their own right too and, if they said, 'Don, let me try this – it may sound better', he would let them and it usually did. So, I may have been some bloke from Scotland they hadn't heard of before but they worked hard to give me the very best album possible. That's what I love about the American attitude. They'd just keep going until they got it right whereas, over here, the attitude was more 'Right, it's time for a break as stated in the Musicians' Union's handbook.' They'd never do that in Nashville.

There was no doubt I was working in the music Mecca of the world. One day, we were in the studios and this guy came in with a guitar, trying to punt songs for my album. What I loved was all the old pros stopped and gave this newcomer the time of day because, at one point, they had probably been in exactly the same position of hawking their wares around the studios in the hope that someone would decide to use one of their songs. So this guy started on the guitar and I'll never forget his song which was called 'Dance with Me Molly'. Not only was his song incredible, his voice was unbelievable too. It was then that I felt like a fake. Here I was – a bloke who could play a bit on guitar, who would like to think he could hold a note or two and who signed to a major record label – and this young fella – who was so talented that he could not only write the most amazing songs but sing them too – was having to tout around the studios for work.

Unfortunately, Don told this boy that we couldn't take his songs because we already had our full quota for my album. He just said, 'No problem, guys, maybe next time – thanks for your time!' and left. His name was Roger Bowling and, shortly after our encounter, he went on to co-write 'Lucille' and 'Coward of the County' for Kenny Rogers – both were worldwide hits and, along with 'Ruby', they are probably the songs Kenny will always be remembered for. It does make you wonder what would have happened if we had been able to use Roger that day – maybe, if we had, he would have eventually offered me those country and western classics instead of giving them to Kenny!

Sadly Roger has since died of a drugs overdose, which is an awful waste, but, seeing how they operate in Nashville, my only surprise is that you don't hear more of that sort of thing going on. Any time I hear his songs on the radio, I always think of that hungry young musician trying to flog me his songs and how I knew I was in the presence of immense talent that day – and how small he made me feel!

It was also interesting to hear how in 2005 – over thirty years after my Nashville album – Cliff Richard went over to record his new album in Tennessee too and came back with a song called 'What Car' which the critics – with even Terry Wogan amongst them – said was Cliff's best work in years. That didn't surprise me in the slightest because Nashville can't fail to inspire you. Their musicians strive for perfection and that raises your game to a whole new level. You may be totally happy with what you've just done but, if there's something that they just don't like – even if it's something they can't quite put their finger on – they will try to sort it by doing something a different way. And, that incredible attention to detail is what makes the end result so good.

At the end of each day, the musicians would all go home, as they were all family men, so there was no socialising. However, Don, the producer, would normally take me to his house. Getting there was usually a hair-raising experience as he was normally doped out of his skull after a day on the weed in the studio. He had this big Mercedes saloon and he stayed on the other side of Nashville – it was like getting into a car with a drunk driver really. Then, to make matters worse, on the journey home, he'd then pop some Valium to try to counteract the effect of the drugs so that his wife and kids didn't know he was wasted. We'd all be seated around the dinner table and all have to join hands and say prayers.

While this was going on, I couldn't help thinking Don was being slightly hypocritical as, just quarter of an hour before, he had been popping Valium after a day on the dope. But it did make me laugh – even though I really hated taking those car rides.

After nearly two months away from home, living out my dream, I returned home with what I was convinced was the best work I had done in my life. Although I was on a high from the whole experience – well, you would be too after spending day after day in a studio filled with dope smoke – I was left feeling disgruntled about the UK music scene, after the professionalism and the whole set up in Nashville. I felt invigorated and was ready to show them all what you could do with hard work and dedication.

My LP, which was simply called *The Nashville Album*, was released with a blaze of publicity and I promoted it on every radio station, TV show and newspaper that I could as I had never been so proud of any album before. Then, to my amazement and that of the bosses of Phonogram, it flopped. Actually, flopped is probably too strong a word but it definitely had the poorest sales of any of my albums. It had cost something like half a million pounds to make and it soon became apparent that the record company were not going to get their money back. It would probably be the beginning of the end for me as far as Phonogram were concerned but, contrary to popular belief, it didn't ruin me. It lost the label money but not me.

I had to look upon it as an experiment that had failed and I must confess it left me feeling deflated and disillusioned. It also made me realise that I had to go back to giving people what they wanted and they most certainly didn't want my Nashville album. They didn't want anything too clever from me. Sometimes, by trying to progress and do something better, you think you're taking steps forward when really you're going backwards.

I knew it was the death knell for any other experiments and I would just have to go back to just doing classic Sydney. I soon picked myself up as you can't allow yourself to be demoralised for too long in this industry and I went back to giving my fans what I knew they liked. Although Nashville had been a commercial disaster, for me personally, it was one of the best experiences of my life – I had been able to do what anyone who sings country and western music wants to do – make an album in Nashville.

18

THE GHOST OF ELVIS

During my time in Nashville, I lived in the same apartment block as Lamar Fike who, would you believe it, was a member of the original Memphis Mafia. When I first met him, Elvis was still alive and, by that point, Lamar had been working for The King as a gofer for about twenty-three years. I got to know him very well and we stayed in touch when I returned home. Shortly after I had met him in 1977, when I was recording my Nashville album, Elvis died on August the 16th of that year at the age of just forty-two.

Exactly twelve months later, Lamar invited me, Shirley and our daughter, Karen, over for the first anniversary of Elvis's death. Now this next part is very freaky and when people read this in the book they'll say, 'Yeah, right, Sydney!' However, before you think I'm telling porkies, bear in mind that I am the most sceptical person on the planet and I certainly don't believe in ghosts. I'm so cynical I have to see things ten times over before I'll believe them. But, let me tell you this, what happened to us in Nashville is inexplicable and it still sends a shiver down my spine to this day.

We were staying in a room in Lamar's Nashville apartment and, on the anniversary of Elvis's death, we flew down to Memphis where we were met at the airport by our big friend Lamar. When I say big, I do mean big – Lamar was around twenty-eight stones. In fact, before he died, Elvis actually paid for Lamar to have his stomach stapled because being so grossly overweight was killing him. Just before we visited him in Nashville, Lamar had flown over to see us in Scotland and he came to one of my gigs at the Kings Theatre in Edinburgh. Seemingly, when you have this stomach op, you have to take about a million pills to keep everything working and, when you go to the toilet, it's like the worst farmyard smells you've ever encountered. I remember the stage door-keeper at the Kings saying to me that Lamar had been to the toilet and he had stunk out the entire theatre. This was no laughing matter – the guy was staying with us!

Anyway, when we went to mark the anniversary of Elvis's death, Lamar was still working at Gracelands and he picked us up in a customised minibus, a really luxurious vehicle. As we approached Gracelands, I swear the queue of fans and cars there was around ten miles long. But, because we were with Lamar, we were allowed to drive straight in through the front gates.

Inside, we were treated to what every Elvis fan dreams of – an unofficial tour of his home during which we got to see the parts no tourist can reach. We saw where all the material was kept for his suits, his stack of motorbikes which were all kept in a shed, his stables of horses, racquet ball courts – the whole thing was just incredible. We got a true feeling for the man and we were so honoured that our host had brought us there. Karen was so moved by it all that she was in floods of tears. Afterwards, we all had a very quiet meal together and reflected on what we had just experienced. We then flew back to Nashville with Lamar and this is where it gets spooky.

Lamar had put us up in a room in his apartment with a bed settee in it. The walls were plastered with framed photographs of Elvis – Elvis with Colonel Tom Parker, Elvis with the President, Elvis with Lamar and then there were others with just Lamar and the likes of Marilyn Monroe. I could have stared at them for hours.

When we had left for Memphis, the door to our room had been open. It had one of those locks you could only secure from the inside, like a bathroom lock. But, when we arrived back, our door was locked from the inside. This was one of these apartment blocks with a security desk and cameras everywhere – there was no way to get in or out without going past security. Lamar immediately panicked, called the guards, ran to a drawer and pulled out a gun. It was like a scene from a movie seeing this twenty-eight-stone guy going berserk with a gun – it had me reaching for the toilet paper. Suddenly the apartment was full of security guards who were also waving guns about the place. It was terrifying and, by this time, Shirley, Karen and I were cowering in a corner.

A guard then booted the locked door to our room down and they all rushed in with their loaded weapons, only to find the room was completely empty. What's more, everything was exactly as we had left it apart from one thing – every photograph of Elvis was squint. There were maybe thirty pictures in that room and all the ones with The King in them were skew-whiff. None of the others with Lamar in them had been touched. Security, by this time, had searched the entire flat and it was empty and no windows or doors had been forced open or anything. The only odd thing they found was a red towelling dressing gown, lying in the middle of Lamar's room. Lamar was very meticulous and he would never dump something in the middle of the floor. But you could have knocked us over when Lamar then told us that the dressing gown had been a present from Presley – and all of this had happened on the first anniversary of Elvis's death . . .

We had been the last ones to leave that apartment and there was no way someone could have slipped in under the noses of the security guards and all the closed circuit TV cameras to do all that. If someone else had been telling me this story I would have found it almost impossible to believe it. But, I'll tell you, it frightened the living daylights out of me because both Shirley and I knew that someone, or something, had been in our room. You could feel a presence and it left us rattled – of course, it didn't help matters that we were also in a strange country with people with guns running around us. That night we got wrecked on whisky as there was no other way we'd have been able to sleep in that room.

So was it the spirit of Elvis? I just don't know. I don't believe in the spirit world or anything like that but something had occurred and, eerily, it just so happens that it had taken place on the anniversary of his death. Maybe it was The King paying me a visit to say, 'That'll teach you to sing my songs, ya Scottish bastard!'

But, if the ghost of Elvis had broken into our room in August of 1978, I also did my own bit of breaking and entering in Nashville in the same year. When I had been recording my Nashville album I had I got very friendly with a fella called George Richey who was a fantastic piano player. I phoned him up when I returned for Elvis's anniversary and he gave me his address and told me to jump in a taxi and come over straightaway. Well, the driveway to his house must have been quarter of a mile long – it was a huge place. When I stepped out of the taxi, I was greeted by the sight of the legendary singer, Tammy Wynette. Apparently news had just broken that my friend George was just about to run off and get married to her – and here she was so it appeared to be true. That's why, when I'd called him, he told me to come over straightaway as they were just about to leave. George shook my hand, asked how I was doing and then casually said, 'This is Tammy.' I'd been lucky enough to meet Tammy a couple of years before at The Apollo in Glasgow and she remembered me as the Scottish country singer. They were desperate to get away to wherever it was they were going to to get married but, in their haste, they'd locked the car keys inside their Cadillac.

They didn't know what to do – but I did. I asked Tammy to go and get me one of her wire coat hangers. I bent it into shape, stuffed it down the window of their Caddy and, hey presto, I got the door open and Tammy and George raced off to get married. I like to consider that as one of my proudest achievements – the day I broke into Tammy Wynette's car so she could go off to get married.

19

GETTING DRUNK WITH
THE JACKSONS

In 1977 I had the great honour of performing at the Royal Performance for the Queen's Silver Jubilee at Glasgow's King's Theatre. Although it would still be a hugely prestigious event today, it would be nothing compared to how it was back then, when being asked to appear was the equivalent of being knighted! It was a huge deal and it was watched by millions across the world.

On the bill that year was Dolly Parton and The Jackson 5. Dolly was absolutely stunning and we hit it off as I knew a lot of the people she'd practically grown up with in Nashville. Despite the fact that we were all pretty experienced performers, the whole occasion was very nerve-wracking and everyone seemed to be on edge. I was standing right beside Dolly when the Queen and Prince Philip were introduced to us. Her Majesty asked me, 'Are you part of the Scottish contingent?' and I said, 'Yes, Ma'am.' She said, 'Thank you very much.' Then she moved on – one was obviously not in the chattiest of moods that evening.

Philip was a different kettle of fish and he blethered with all of us. The Prince had grabbed Dolly's hand to shake it but her dress was actually attached to her fingers by a string of rhinestones so, when Philip squeezed her hand, she grimaced as the rhinestones dug in and he apologised. I have a photo where you can see Dolly looking down at her hand after he squeezed it. I was next in line and I was standing there in my black leather suit which also had rhinestones on it. Philip turned to me and said, 'You'll be more used to this than I am.' I glanced along at the Queen and said, 'Er, excuse me, Sir, but I think *you*'ll be more used it to than I am!' I was, of course, referring to the fact that the Queen never went anywhere without all her baubles on and he burst out laughing.

After the show, I was so relieved everything had gone so well that I couldn't wait to unwind with a drink. I was up in my dressing room, which I was sharing with Lionel Blair and the Scottish entertainer Allan Stewart, when there was a knock at the door and The Jackson 5 were standing there. Actually, Michael wasn't with them at that moment so it was more like The Jackson 4 and they were all big strapping young men. Being a good host, I asked if they fancied trying some whisky. They asked how to drink it and I told them that Scotsmen always drink it neat. Well, it was like feeding firewater to the Indians – they couldn't get enough of the stuff. In later years, I heard how their father was a bit of a control freak but that night Daddy was looking after the youngest brother, Michael, so it meant the older siblings were off the leash and, boy, did they love it.

It's fair to say The Jacksons were highly delighted with the Scottish hospitality as they got stuck into two bottles of Johnny Walker Black Label. We all had a great night as Allan and Lionel and I exchanged stories and these big Jackson boys set about demolishing the local tipple. So I never got to meet the young Michael who would go on to be probably the biggest star in the world but I don't think his brothers will ever forget the Scotsman who got them completely sozzled after their audience with the Queen.

145

20

THE DEVINE DRUG RUNNERS

In 1983, when our youngest, Scot was ten, Shirley and I decided to join him on a school skiing holiday to France. All the parents from Drumlay House School in Mossblown were invited along and we thought it would be a nice experience to do some skiing while Scot enjoyed himself with his friends.

Shortly before our trip, we were at a dinner party with Harvey Davidson, a businessman who owned Parasol Holidays which was based in Glasgow's Giffnock area. I mentioned to him that we were going on this skiing holiday with my son's school and one of the other guests was a guy who worked in customs at Glasgow Airport. This fella told me I could use the staff car park at the airport instead of booking my car into the long-stay car park. I was very grateful as this car park was much closer to the terminal which would be very handy with so much ski equipment to lug about.

We spent a magnificent week skiing in marvellous conditions and we got back to Glasgow Airport in high spirits. But, unfortunately, when we went to collect our bags at the luggage carousel, we discovered that one of our ski-boot bags was missing. I said to Shirley and Scot that we should just go and load the car up with what luggage we had and then come back to report that our bag was missing. We loaded the car up, got inside and were just about to start it up to drive back to the terminal when, suddenly, my door flew open and I saw about twenty customs' officers surrounding the car. They then ordered me to get out. I'm not kidding – it was like a commando raid. One of them said, 'Right, Mr Devine, come with us.' So my son, Shirley and I all trooped back to customs where they took our cases and examined everything inside them – and I mean everything.

I asked them, 'What's happening here?' And one of them smirked and said, 'Don't tell me you don't know, Mr Devine.' I said, 'You're right, I don't know. I haven't got a clue why we're in here. Is it about the missing bag?' But they never answered me. I was then asked why I was parked in the staff car park. I explained how I'd met one of their colleagues at a dinner party but they didn't seem to be listening to what I was saying by this point as they were so intent on looking for something. By now, they were even squeezing my toothpaste out of the tube.

One of these customs' officers – officer is probably too polite a word for him, idiot is a lot more appropriate – then picked up a Styptic, a kind of pencil which stops you bleeding if you nick yourself shaving. The one I had was American and it was shaped like a long, thick cigar. This customs' officer spotted it and thought he'd hit the jackpot. He opened the lid and licked it. God knows what it must of tasted like but this customs' man's face grimaced in revulsion. While they were painstakingly going through my stuff, they were also doing the same to Shirley's luggage but, strangely, these Brains of Britain didn't touch any of Scot's stuff. If we were running drugs, which was obviously what they thought we were doing, then we could have easily packed the ten-year-old's case with the stuff and they didn't even look at his bags.

This whole process took four hours and, just when we thought the ordeal was coming to an end, they ordered Shirley and me into separate rooms for a strip-search. Poor Scot was so upset at having his mummy and daddy taken away from him but I told him not to worry and everything would be all right. Well, it wasn't all right. Shirley and I were subjected to the most degrading and humiliating experience of our lives as they inspected every orifice of our bodies.

After this, I was reduced to pleading with them. 'Why are you doing all this? Why are you doing this to my wife? Why are you upsetting my son?' I asked them. All they said was that they had received information that suggested we were carrying some illegal substance. We had no choice but to cooperate and, at one point, an officer said to us, 'You're being remarkably nice about all this.' That just made me angry. I told them it would be the last time they ever got to lay a finger on us and next time they could deal with my lawyer. I also said that, if there was to be any physical examinations, they would be carried out by my own doctor, not theirs, because I didn't trust them or their motives.

Of course, they didn't find anything and, afterwards, I hugged Shirley who just broke down into floods of tears. To add insult to injury, we had about a bottle and a half of spirits over the duty-free limit and, instead of letting us go after what they had put us through, they made sure they charged us the extra duty. Next, they looked at my watch and asked if I had a receipt for it. I said, 'Not on me but I can give you the number of the jeweller's in Ayr where I bought it, if you like.' At that moment, they knew they had nothing and they were clutching at straws. They were desperate to find something, anything at all, to justify their over-the-top actions. You have to be a special kind of person to do all that to an innocent family.

For months afterwards, I churned the whole scenario over and over in my mind and still couldn't make head nor tail of it. I don't think it could have stemmed from the officer I met at the dinner party but I do think it was something to do with someone in the school party – not a teacher or a pupil but one of the parents. I have no proof whatsoever – it's just a gut instinct. While we were on the trip, I felt that this person had taken a dislike to me. I think it might have stemmed from a bit of jealousy but I'm not sure. If I'm right, they must have really hated me to have spent all that time and energy tipping off the authorities back home because one thing's for certain – they were waiting for us.

Now what kind of lowlife scum would do that to another human being just because they didn't like them? I had never insulted this person or had a cross word with them but you can always tell when someone doesn't like you. Instead of being a man about it and saying it to my face, they had to be sneaky and underhand. Well, I don't mind someone having a go at me but what that scumbag did left Shirley in tears and she remembers the humiliation to this day. I hope that person can look at their reflection in the mirror and be happy with what they see.

What makes me even angrier is the fact that one malicious person can make an anonymous tip-off and put innocent people through such a harrowing ordeal.

There were further repercussions to come because, for about two weeks after the incident at Glasgow Airport, my phone was tapped. I have no doubt about it – people were most definitely listening to my conversations. I could just tell because, when I lifted the phone, there would be some activity before I'd get a dial tone and, at other times, I could hear voices. That stopped after a fortnight but then, every time I went through Glasgow Airport for the next two years, they would pull me over. At one point, I got so sick of it I complained that they were deliberately targeting me and, after that, it came to an end.

We used to have customs' officers staying at our B&B in Prestwick and we always got on well with them but, after the ordeal they put us through, I'll never forgive them. They made a tax-paying, law-abiding person like myself resentful of everything they stand for and, as a result, I would never cooperate with them again.

Surprisingly, this story never came out in the press at the time and I was certainly too hurt to talk about it but I had a feeling that the customs' men would have been delighted to have successfully targeted a high-profile scalp like mine. Well, guys, I do music – not drugs. I never have and never will. So how about targeting some of the real bad boys next time instead of terrifying an innocent family?

21

NEGATIVE STORIES

Now when you've been around as long as I have – and, let's face it, there aren't too many on the scene today who can boast of over fifty years in showbiz – it's only natural that there will be some negative press. Fortunately for me, over the years, there hasn't been too much and I've always had the attitude that, if you're going to court the press in order to sell a single, an album, a concert, a line-dancing video or whatever, then you can't go complaining when they print something you don't like.

One thing I do object to, however, is when my name is used in vain in a sports report or something. You know the kind of thing – 'The Kilmarnock defence was as bad as a Sydney Devine show.' I suppose, because of my stage outfits and style, I am an easy target and anyone who has been around over the decades, from Des O'Connor to The Krankies, will always find themselves a target for this type of thing. I honestly have no problem with that – I think anybody has the right to take the Mickey. What I do object to is when it amounts to disrespect. I don't think anyone has the right to criticise me unless they've been to one of my shows. If, after that, they say that I'm crap, then fair enough. Fortunately, all those who come to see me at The Pavilion every year don't seem to think I'm crap and they're the ones who matter because they pay my wages.

Aside from popping up in the occasional sports report, I have also hit the headlines for another reason. It's one vice that I find very hard to kick – speeding. I have always lived life within the rules of the law except when it comes to fast cars – then I just can't help myself. However irresponsible this may sound, I just find it so difficult to sit on a motorway at 70mph in a car that's capable of doing more than twice that.

The first time I was done for speeding and hit the headlines was in the summer of 1984. I had just finished playing my own show at Turnberry when Dick Condon from The Theatre Royal in Norwich called. This was on the Saturday night and he was desperate for me to do a show on Sunday. And it wasn't an evening performance he was after – he needed me for the matinee. I was happy to do it for Dick as he was a great guy and probably the most incredible salesman I've ever met. He took something like five per cent of your merchandise sales but the beauty was that he sold it for you and, boy, was he good at flogging your wares to the punters. He would stand at the front of the theatre and tell folk that they weren't allowed in unless they bought my records. Once, we were selling sticks of rock and he was shouting, 'Buy Sydney's rock – you can suck on Sydney's rock all night long!' He was crude but effective.

So I agreed to do the show in Norwich. I was taking my guitarist, Owen Knox, with me and I decided we'd have to leave at six in the morning. Even with such an early start, I knew I'd have to floor it in my Mercedes Benz 500 SLK sports car. On the way to Norwich, I was stopped for speeding not once but twice. Being well used to dealing with traffic cops by this time, I wasn't too bothered when the police car stopped me because I noticed there was only one policeman in it and, in Scotland, there needs to be at least two officers to charge a speeding driver. However, I was in Lincolnshire at the time and I had no idea it was different in England – one cop was enough to have you busted.

He asked where I was going and if I was in entertainment but I reckon he already knew who I was from my car registration 9 SYD. He then said, 'Well, unfortunately, Mr Devine, you were speeding – you were doing 53mph in a 30mph limit.' I did the usual 'I'm so very sorry' routine, still thinking that he's not in a position to actually charge me. But, then he started reading the procedure, saying I have to present my licence at the Crown Prosecution Service. By this time, the guitarist's shoulders were bobbing up and down and he was trying to hold back from bursting out laughing and, all the time, the cop was still droning on, 'which may lead to criminal proceedings . . .' And it didn't stop there. He continued, 'Oh and, by the way, you were also doing 89mph in a 70mph limit . . . you should present your licence . . . this may lead to criminal proceedings . . .' I asked him why he hadn't stopped me the first time he'd seen me speeding and he said, 'Because I knew I could get you twice.' He had seen the sports car, noticed it had a private reg and thought, 'I'll have him.' Then, to top it all, the bastard asked why I've never played in Lincoln because he'd like to come and see me. I just told him I'd probably find it too expensive to drive there!

So, over the years, I've been done quite a few times and I finally lost my licence in 1990 after speeding on the Irvine–Ayr bypass. I'd been out fishing and had arranged to do a benefit gig for Marie Curie Cancer Care later that day so I was tanning it to get there in time. Ironically, it was an English cop again who got me. I gave him all the chat and told him I'd been fishing but I had left it a bit late to get home, get changed and go to the charity concert. He said, 'That may be so,

Mr Devine, but you were doing 106 miles per hour when you overtook us.'

I pled guilt by letter but the sheriff didn't want that and ordered me to appear before Kilmarnock Sheriff Court. The sheriff obviously wanted his bit of glory and his mention in the paper. Of course, when I turned up, all the TV cameras and newspaper photographers were there. So I had my licence taken off me for three months, got fined £500 *and* I was humiliated in public. Shirley had to do all the driving during the time I was disqualified and, although she is an excellent driver, it was murder being without my wheels. I think that was when I finally realised I couldn't drive the way I had always done in the past.

However, I must admit that I have been let off more times than I've actually been charged and, on those occasions when they didn't do me, I think I probably should have been booked. Most of the cops just gave me a ticking-off and said, 'Will you accept a warning, Mr Devine?' After a sigh of relief, I'd be only to happy to reply, 'You're damn right I will.'

One of the most bizarre stories involving the cops, though, was when I was charged with breach of the peace at a posh party. In 1985, after a show at Ayr's Gaiety Theatre, I had gone to this party in the town. As usual, I hadn't left the theatre until eleven at night so, when I got to the do, it was catch-up time. I got talking to Glen Henderson, a local car dealer but, having had a drink on an empty stomach – you know the old story about 'when the drink's in, the wit's out' – the booze seemed to hit me hard. Before I knew it, we were involved in a bit of an argument. I seem to remember it started when Glen said to me, 'You'll be buying your Mercedes Benz from me in future.' I told him that I always bought my Mercs from Callanders in Glasgow so some more words were exchanged and these were followed by a fist being thrown and that first punch didn't come from me. Even though I was a bit tipsy and possibly slightly argumentative, I knew better than to take on a six-foot-three-inch ex-champion ice skater when I'm only five-foot-seven-and-a-half-inch tall. On top of being charged with breach of the peace, I was left with a broken nose and a badly dented ego. The ironic thing was that, at one point, I did end up buying cars from Glen – although I would never say we were friends.

Luckily, the breach of the peace charge was later dropped but the papers seemed to carry it for weeks. My attitude has always been one of there's no such thing as bad publicity and, if you're fed up reading your press cuttings, then you should just weigh them instead. However, sometimes you can be dragged into a newspaper story even when it has nothing to do with you at all and that has happened to me on a number of occasions.

During the 1980s, my poor sister, Jean, was described as 'Sydney's Sister from Hell' in *The Sun* newspaper. As it turned out, she was apparently being branded a nuisance neighbour. Now, my Jean was really more to be pitied than talked about because she had a massive drink problem. She was an alcoholic and alcoholism is a disease so it's tragic that she was painted out to be such a horrible person in the paper because that wasn't the Jean I knew. She wasn't well but she had a good heart and was a truly nice person. Of course, if the headline had been 'Jean Murray, Neighbour from Hell', it wouldn't have had any impact at all – it would have been a story that wouldn't have meant anything to anyone. But, by making it about Sydney Devine's sister, they had their screaming headline and a hint of scandal – they were saying, 'Look, that Sydney Devine's living the high life while his sister's destitute.' But I'm not my sister's keeper. I understand that there is now an editor's code of conduct which means that newspapers are not supposed to print a story about a person unless that person actually features prominently in the story – it's effectively a kind of ban on printing stuff that involves fame by association – but I doubt it will stop them.

Then the *Sunday Mail*, normally one of my greatest supporters, ran the headline 'Sydney's Grandson Living in a Caravan'. The thrust of the story was that I was being such a meanie for allowing my grandson, Ben, to live in poverty. The truth was that my son, Gary, and his wife, Tracey, had split up and, I suppose out of revenge or whatever, Tracey went to the newspaper, saying they were living in a mobile home. I knew absolutely nothing about this. Again, here I was, big bad Sydney, being dragged into something that was nothing to do with me. People get divorced all the time and no one was sadder than I was when Gary and Tracey split up because I hated the thought of my grandson being upset by it.

Eventually, I had to laugh at the whole ridiculous story, though. Tracey's family, the Spiers, were scrap dealers and, as everyone knows, 'scrappies' are never short of a few quid. In the *Sunday Mail* photograph, Tracey is, indeed, sitting there in a caravan but, as we later found out, it was at the bottom of the garden at her parents' house. And, if you look closely at the picture, although she looks like a waif, she has two rings on her fingers which were probably worth the best part of £10,000–£15,000 – and she was claiming to be living in destitution! The irony is that Gary and Tracey are now on friendly terms and I honestly bear no grudge for what she did as I'm sure she had her reasons at the time. Shirley and I always got on well with her – she is the mother of our grandchild after all – and I wish her nothing but the best.

Please don't think I'm up on my high horse over this. I appreciate that the papers have helped make me what I am today and you have to take the rough with the smooth – it's just part and parcel of the business. Take the Beckhams, for instance. They court the media by lunching with newspaper editors to get them to publicise David's endorsement of a new pair of football boots or plug Victoria's latest single in an attempt to improve her dwindling record sales. Then they try to take out court injunctions when the papers want to print stories that they don't like. That's plain stupid.

And how do people know the truth anyway? I mean the papers never asked me if I tried to help my poor alcoholic sister or my daughter in law. If they had, I might have told them that I have helped both of them out financially – and not with small sums of money either. But the papers wouldn't be interested in that – it would kind of ruin their stories. They want to concentrate on the idea that I'm living it up while members of my family are suffering.

With regard to the media, what I do think is sad is that there isn't enough good news in the world or, if there is, it tends to be ignored in favour of lurid headlines.

22

HOW I HELPED TO MAKE LENA ZAVARONI A STAR

One day I was doing some voice-overs at Chappels Studios in London with my record producer, Tommy Scott, and he told me he'd just met this wee nine-year-old girl from Rothesay. Tommy told me her name was Lena Zavaroni and he said, 'You've never heard a voice like this before in your life but we're struggling for the right song for her.' I agreed that certain songs are just not suitable for little kids to sing. I told Tommy that I remembered the Johnny Otis Show Band did a song called 'Ma, He's Making Eyes at Me' and, although its subject is flirtation, it deals with it playfully and I thought it might be a good number for Lena.

About five months later, I was down doing the final voices on my album when Tommy said, 'Listen to this!' and he put on Lena's record. I immediately thought, 'God Almighty, who's that?', completely forgetting our previous conversation. Tommy said, 'That's the wee lassie from Rothesay I was telling you about – only she's ten years old now.' I just couldn't believe that any ten-year-old could have a voice like that. Tommy asked, 'What do you think?' and I immediately said, 'That's a number one, Tommy – in fact, I'm so confident that I'll bet you a fiver she'll top the charts.' Needless to say. I'm still waiting for my money.

It was the perfect song for Lena and I'm glad I was the person who helped get her to number one. I would later have Lena on my STV show *Devine Time* – she was a great wee performer and a lovely lassie. I saw her a few times after that and, just like everyone else in the business, I was appalled at how her life turned out – she died in 1999 at the age of just thirty-five, having battled with the eating disorder anorexia for twenty-two years.

Funnily enough, Lena's management team were the Solomons – the same people I had signed my infamous Emerald recording contract with. Mervyn Solomon ran Emerald and his brother Phil's wife, Dorothy, was Lena's manager. I remember being in the canteen at STV, during the recording of *Devine Time*, when Dorothy curtly said to me, 'Sydney, don't smoke in front of Lena!' I told Dorothy, 'If you don't want to sit at this table, go and sit somewhere else!' which she did. Dorothy thought she could order everyone about and that's the way she treated Lena all the time. It was always, 'You can't have this, Lena' or 'You can't have that, Lena' 'Don't eat those biscuits, Lena' or 'Don't eat those crisps, Lena – you're too fat!' Now Lena was maybe about twelve or thirteen when she did my show and, like most boys and girls of that age, she had some puppy fat. She was by no means chubby – she was just a normal young girl. I felt so sorry for her because it meant she just didn't have a life. I saw it with my own eyes and I didn't like what I witnessed. Lena had had enough to cope with at the time – having been taken away from her folks at such an early age – without being continually told what she could and couldn't eat.

Now, there is no way I could say that the way she was treated back then was the direct cause of her eating disorder but I'm sure it couldn't have helped much. Her whole life was tragic and it was horrendous to see her in later years become so painfully thin. I just wish she had had better guidance – the kind of people Charlotte Church has had. To me, Lena was a far bigger talent than Charlotte and she had a much better voice. She was a classic Scottish belter and, had she been around and healthy today, I'm sure she would have been a mega, mega star as I think her voice would have got even better the older she got. But, because she was an instant success at such a young age, all of a sudden, people were jumping on the bandwagon to make a quick buck. They don't see the long game – it's just all about getting as much money out of a person while it lasts. So poor Lena missed all her youth and her teenage years, which are very important in anybody's life as they shape you.

I have often thought maybe things would have turned out differently if I hadn't recommended 'Ma, He's Making Eyes at Me' but you can't think like that and I will always have the memory of that wee girl's voice leaving me almost lost for words the moment I heard her.

23

THE DEVINE AIRWAVES

I was at Radio Clyde for ten years and loved every minute of it. I worked with some of the best people in the business and also got to meet some rather interesting people – like Sheena Easton. She'd just recorded '9 to 5', the hit she had straight after appearing on the Esther Rantzen show *The Big Time*. Sheena was doing the rounds of radio stations when she came in to Clyde. I was sitting in the canteen and we got talking. I offered her just one piece of advice. I said, 'Just watch out, Sheena. This is quite a hard game. It's a hard game for anybody but it's a harder game for a young lady, especially one with a voice as good as yours.' But I will always remember the way she looked me straight in the eyes and coolly said, 'Oh, don't you worry about me, Sydney, I'm going to make it.' At first I thought, 'What a big head' – but she didn't half make it and she always knew she would.

Some people's success just happens to them by accident – like mine did – but Sheena chased after it. There was no doubt about it and she did it with the confidence of someone who knew she was going to be big. However, even though she has millions and all that, I wonder if she really knows who she is. I mean, shortly after we met, her Scottish accent went and she ditched her husband – the first of many. It's good to see she's looked after the shekels but, from my point of view, she was a great talent who lost her way. She didn't have to adopt this mid-Atlantic accent just to be a success – after all,

SIMPLY DEVINE

Sean Connery never changed his accent and, in fact, it became his biggest asset. I believe it's a great pity that some people find it necessary to try to cover up their roots because there are two things you should never ever forget – who you are and where you come from. It's a hard road on the way up but it's a rolling stone on the way back down.

Anyway, back to radio, it has been said I had left Clyde acrimoniously but that isn't true – I left to go to their then rivals WestSound. Based in Ayr, they were offering a similar deal to the one I was on at Clyde – same wages – but they were on my doorstep and that meant I didn't have to make that treacherous journey up the A77 every weekend. I went on to do another ten years at WestSound but, when I left there, it *was* with a cloud hanging over me.

The reason for my departure was that they said they were losing audiences but I simply don't believe that. Things had started to change at WestSound. They started broadcasting to Stranraer but had lots of technical problems making the switch. I won't bore you with the ins and outs but they had set up the most stupid system I've ever seen. It basically meant that someone sitting down in Stranraer listening to the *Sydney Devine Show* would maybe get about two minutes of dead air every ten minutes – it was a nightmare. So Gordon McArthur, who was the manager of WestSound at that time, said to me one morning, 'Can I see you after your programme finishes?'

Now, Gordon was also a newsreader although I use that term loosely. I'm not being facetious but what he did for the news was the equivalent of what that iceberg did for the *Titanic*. I just couldn't understand a word he said – he must have been one of the worst newsreaders on any radio programme ever. After I finished my show, I went to see him and he started acting the big shot. He said, 'We've got a little problem here – we're losing figures.' I said, 'They may have dropped in Stranraer but that's because you manage to give them about twelve minutes of dead air every hour – my figures will be fine everywhere else.' And I then asked him, 'Are you using this as an excuse or is there something else?' but I never got an answer. I then asked, 'Would you find it easier if I just went?' and Gordon said, 'Well, tell me how you feel'. I told him, 'I feel like I won't bother coming in on Sunday.' And that was it – I left there and then without getting a chance to say goodbye to all my loyal listeners.

I think there was another agenda, though, as what was really behind it was that Radio Clyde were just about to buy out WestSound and I think the powers that be at Clyde were either still a bit peeved that I had left them or they simply didn't fancy having me do a show any more. I never found out what was going on and I think now I'll never know. It's a pity, though, because I loved doing radio. It wasn't just the buzz I enjoyed about broadcasting, it was the ability to actually do things and make a wee bit of a difference – like all the fundraising I did over the airwaves for Erskine Hospital. I'd ask listeners to send me a pound and, in return, I'd play their requests. I did the same to help the pensioners at Christmas – send in a pound, get your request played on the radio and the money goes to make sure elderly folk have a better Christmas. We gave a lot of money to Erskine over the years and we made many pensioners in the West of Scotland happy over the festive time too.

But all that came to an end and no one ever did anything like that again on air at WestSound. For that reason alone I feel sorry that it all came to an end.

24

MY HEART ATTACK

Probably all of us, at some point, have taken our health for granted – I suppose it's only human nature. It's a pity that we only truly begin to treat our bodies properly when they start to go wrong. What happened to me in 1989 would shape the rest of my life.

It began on a Friday morning. I had my one-and-a-half-year-old grandson, Ryan, in my arms in the hallway. He was always a big boy but, this particular day, I couldn't believe how heavy he felt. As I was holding him, it just felt like he was getting heavier and heavier. Being a heavy smoker at the time, the first thing I instinctively did was light up a cigarette – bonkers, I know. So there I was standing smoking in the kitchen and not even enjoying it, which must have been a first, so I put the cigarette, which was nearly whole, out.

Then Shirley came in and asked if there was anything wrong. That's the great thing about being married to someone for a while – they can spot when something's wrong immediately. I told her that I was going up to bed and this was something that, in itself, was pretty strange. I then slumped on to the bed and lay there face down. I remember thinking this was a first as I've never lain face down any time in my life. Shirley was very concerned but I just told her I was having a bout of bad heartburn. Unbeknown to me, Shirley had nipped off and phoned the doctor. I got up as I simply couldn't settle, went back downstairs and relit my cigarette. All the time, the pain in my chest was getting worse and worse. I was extremely agitated and couldn't rest. I'd never felt like that in my life so decided to try to lie down on the bed again.

Shortly after this, a doctor I'd never seen before arrived. He was an ex-army man called Steven Glen – a very smart young man. He was extremely calm and gave me a good check-over. He took my pulse and then put a Venflon in my arm – a little cannula (a tiny tube that allows doctors to put medication directly into a vein or take blood samples directly from a vein) with a little cap on the end – as he said that it would give the hospital instant access as they'd need to run some tests. I said, 'I can't go to hospital – I've got WestSound tomorrow morning.' He kind of chuckled and said, 'Mr Devine, you won't be at WestSound tomorrow, believe me.'

He then phoned Heathfield Hospital and told them he had a forty-nine-year-old male patient suffering from severe chest pains and he wanted them to admit the man. It was surreal and it took me a minute to realise it was actually me he was talking about. The staff at Heathfield said they were sorry but they had no beds. He then phoned Ballochmyle and got the same thing again – sorry, no beds. The response from Ayr Hospital was the same. I looked at the doc and said to him, 'Here's me lying in my bed dying and nobody wants me.' Fortunately, it was a case of fourth time lucky and Crosshouse Hospital in Kilmarnock said they could admit me.

The doctor had given me an injection which, seemingly, stops you from doing any more damage to the heart and, by this point, I had started to feel very strange. It was the weirdest thing. A sensation started in my head and moved right down to my toes – it's what I imagine a drugs rush would be like. I began to lose track of time but, before I knew it, an ambulance had arrived and the medics had me strapped into a chair. Soon they were lifting me downstairs and into the back of the ambulance. They had put an oxygen mask on me and the mask was over my face but there was nothing coming out of it and I couldn't breath. I began to think that, between the hospitals not wanting to take me and the ambulance men and their faulty oxygen mask, there was a conspiracy to kill me going on.

The more time passed, the more and more detached I was becoming but I'm sure I heard someone mention on the ambulance radio that they were bringing in Sydney Devine. By the time I reached the hospital in Kilmarnock, I was pretty out of it. Inside, I was met by a consultant, a Mr Groden, who said, 'Hello, Sydney, nice to meet you again.' I was becoming deeply confused. My head was in a daze and here I was in hospital with some bloke claiming he knew me. Suddenly, I had a flash of clarity and remembered that I had done a lot of fundraising for a Jewish charity called The Gardens of Wizo for Patricia Groden, whose husband, Bernard, was a heart consultant. Now, here he was looking after me. The rest is a bit of a blur as I flitted in and out of sleep. I woke up late during my first night there, only to hear a voice coming from the next bed, saying, 'Clear!' The doctors and nurses were obviously trying to kick-start somebody's heart and it was at that point that I started to become frightened as I don't think I had realised how serious a predicament I was in.

I hadn't been that scared since Jimmy Shand Jr tried to drown me in Australia. Fortunately, the panic didn't last too long as whatever drugs they had me on soon knocked me out again. I woke maybe half an hour later to the sound of people crying before drifting off for who knows how long.

Then, like the rerun of a bad dream, I awoke again to sounds coming from another bed – 'Clear . . .' 'Clear . . .' 'Clear . . .' – and then nothing but the sounds of crying as another patient's family came in to say goodbye and pay their last respects.

So, during my first night in hospital, two people died in the beds beside me and it made me even more frightened and scared. I became terrified to go to sleep in case I was next. But, before I knew what was happening, I had drifted off again – the medication I was on never allowed me much conscious time. I suppose all the medicine and painkillers they were pumping into me was a blessing as it stopped me from dwelling on what could happen to me.

I was in Crosshouse for about a week and they were very good to me. They got me a room on my own and managed to keep the outside world from getting in. By this point, there were newspaper journalists and cameramen and TV crews outside the hospital, along with hundreds of fans, but I knew nothing of this until later. When I was eventually released, I went home and did absolutely nothing for two weeks before going back for further tests. I had to walk on a treadmill, while hooked up to all these monitors and the tests must have lasted about a minute and a half. It's funny what your mind will hold on to because, all the time I was doing the tests, there was only one thing worrying me – whether I would still be able to go on a skiing trip with my younger son, Scot. I even asked the nurse after the tests were done what she thought my chances were but she just told me to speak to my consultant, David O'Neill, about it. I then told her, 'The only reason I'm asking is that I promised to take my son skiing and I've already booked it.' She asked where we were going and I told her France. She then said, 'Let's put it this way, Mr Devine, I don't think you'll even be allowed to fly let alone ski.' It was as if I had been hit by a ton of bricks.

Maybe, up until that point, I had been kidding myself on that it wasn't that serious but now I knew I was really in big trouble. I phoned Shirley and I burst out crying and told her that things were a little worse than I thought.

David O'Neill then booked me into Glasgow's Western Infirmary to put a tiny little camera into my groin. From there, it would travel up my body and into my heart to see what damage had been done. They reckoned that two, maybe three, arteries were affected and they would need to be fixed. A few weeks later, I spoke to the surgeon, Morgan Jamieson, who was going to be doing the operation. He went through the whole procedure and told me I stood a good chance of recovery as I looked in fairly good health. He was also pleased to hear that I had managed to stop smoking, which I had – on the very day of my heart attack.

At this point, I told the surgeon that I had BUPA health insurance as I supposed that this would mean I could have the operation done almost immediately. He said, 'Yes, you could but I don't do private.' I admired him for that. He didn't chastise me at all and said, by all means, if I wanted to go private, then I could go to Ross Hall, in Glasgow, but he did warn me that, if anything went wrong during the operation, I'd be brought to the Western anyway. He told me the waiting list was only around twelve weeks and added, 'If I were you, Mr Devine, I'd just go home and take it nice and easy and, as soon as we get a bed, we'll give you call.' He was true to his word and, almost twelve weeks to the day, I went up to the Western for open-heart surgery.

Now, the Western may have been just about the most antiquated-looking hospital I'd ever seen but I would come to think of it as the most wonderful place I've ever been in, in my life. However, no matter how good the care from the staff was, it didn't stop me worrying, especially since, just months before my heart attack, Bernard Cotton, the manager of Ayr's Gaiety Theatre, had popped into my house for a cup of tea and had gone through every gory detail of his own bypass op. Oh, he was a right cheery soul that day as he told me at great length how the surgeon had slit him open at the front and had then cracked his ribs to get into the chest cavity. He then told me how the surgeon had taken his heart out to mend it while his body was lying on a bed of ice. I remember saying to him, 'Well, I hope I never have to go through that.' But I really needn't have worried too much as the care I received in the Western was second to none.

I remember, the morning I was going down to theatre, there was this little doctor from Papworth who was going to be doing the stitching job on my chest after the op. I said to him, 'I want you to promise you'll make a good job of this because I wear a lot of open neck shirts and I don't want to see a giant welder's mark down the front.' Well, he was as good as his word and did an incredible job on me as you can hardly see my scar now.

After surgery, I was able to come off the ventilator just two hours later. It apparently takes most people twenty-four hours to breath on their own but, because I had been singing for so many years, my lungs were very well developed. So, instead of being in intensive care, I was soon back on the ward. Shirley reckons she knew I was going to be OK the minute she saw me. And I knew I felt better myself when I started looking at the nurses' legs! This was in the days before nurses wore trousers or, as I like to think of them, the glory days of nursing. I remember saying to the night nurse,

'Give me a kiss, then!' and she said, 'No, I can't – I shouldn't even be in bed with you!' OK, that was wishful thinking but at least I was certainly feeling perkier. And then, one day, I had a bizarre conversation with a patient on the ward. He told me he was from Ayr but he had a strange accent – it sounded to me like a mix of Mediterranean and Eastern European. I said, 'Well, I live in Ayr and I've never heard a local dialect quite like yours.' It turned out he lived in Ayr but he was from Transylvania. I turned to the other patients and said, 'If you see Bram Stoker here moving towards my bed in the middle of the night, please ring that bell for the nurses!' It's very difficult to laugh when you're in a fair bit of discomfort from all the stitches and tubes but we all managed a giggle that day.

The next day Bram was going home so I very kindly volunteered my wife to drop him off in Ayr. I'm not kidding, the guy really was like something from a Dracula movie and Shirley gave me a look that could kill – I'm the greatest in the world for volunteering tasks for oor Shirley!

But, even though I was starting to feel frisky, there wasn't a lot I could do about it as I had all these tubes and things in me – there were drains coming out my neck and stomach and a catheter in my you-know-what. But, on the third day, I got up and had a shower and I began walking around with these ridiculous white tights they made me wear. Apparently, walking eight times round the ward was equivalent to one mile and I was soon able to complete that.

One morning Morgan Jamieson was working over at York-hill or somewhere and a Mr Bain was doing his morning rounds instead. He came over to my bed and said, 'Ah, Mr Devine, I've been really anxious to listen to these singer's lungs they've all been telling me about.' As he bent over me with his stethoscope, I quickly realised he was reeking of fags. Here was a thoracic professor, a man whose job is to take people's hearts and lungs out because they've smoked too many cigarettes, and he's stinking of cigarettes. Now, if he's seeing the damage smoking does to your insides every day and he can't give up, it's no wonder so many ordinary people struggle to do it.

The response from my fans during this time was incredible and they sent so many bouquets of flowers that the place was like a florist's. When I was finally released, ten days later, I was met at the hospital doors by Ross Wilson, a reporter on the *Daily Record*. I've met a lot of journalists over the years but Ross was definitely one of the nicest of the lot. We did an interview and some photos at the hospital before Shirley drove me back home. The funny thing is that I could not stop crying from the moment we passed through the hospital gates for the entire journey down to Ayr. Seemingly, this is quite a common reaction. It's something to do with the fact that you have survived. They can cure you physically but the mental side of things isn't so easy to fix and your mind doesn't half play havoc with you. It left me feeling so frightened and vulnerable. My mind told me that every twinge – and, to this day, I still get a lot of twinges – was the start of another heart attack.

In my head, I kept churning over a conversation I'd had with Morgan Jamieson about how long the operation would last, how much more time I had left, whether I would be good for maybe another eight, nine, ten years of life . . . but he simply said, 'Don't go down that road.' The truth is that no one knows how long something like an operation to repair a damaged heart is going to last. I went back for a check-up in 2005 and was told that my heart was in excellent condition. So, as far as I'm concerned, Morgan did a phenomenal job and has, so far, extended my life by at least sixteen years and counting.

If you think of it in real terms I should have been dead. Some people who have heart attacks don't survive them and others don't recover even after the operation. Then there's the folk who survive but whose standard of living is so poor because they can't even have any surgery as the wall of their heart is so badly damaged. So I was lucky in two respects – one, that I survived it and, two, that my heart wasn't so badly damaged that they couldn't operate on it.

After the operation, every tour I did was billed as Sydney's farewell performance as rumours were rife I was going to retire. I've had more farewells than Sinatra and was still doing goodbye concerts at The Pavilion in 2000!

I still fish, play golf, garden and ski but, at the back of my mind, it's always there and always will be. There are times when I get some pains actually in my heart and I think it could be the grafts just stretching or whatever. For the minute or so that they last for, I'm thinking, 'Oh, Jesus! This could be the big one.' It's as if someone has taken a knife and thrust it right into my chest and I get crackers like that about once every three months or so. It goes away as quickly as it comes but it acts as a little reminder that perhaps I'm on borrowed time. But the way I look at it is that I've had sixteen years of bonus time.

This is maybe a ridiculous thing to say but it wouldn't bother me if I died tomorrow. I've had such a fantastic life that the only thing I'd hate would be leaving my family behind because I love them dearly and they all love me and I'm very lucky that way. But I'd rather go quickly as my real fear is that, if I have another heart attack, I could end up wheelchair bound. For someone as active as I am, that would be worse than death. In fact, my ideal place to die would be onstage at The Pavilion – well, it wouldn't be the first stage I've died on! But seriously, for me, that would be the perfect send-off. To drop dead after a sell-out show at my favourite theatre – please, God, I hope that's the way I check out.

After the heart attack, I actually seemed to be busier than ever and I finally got to appear in Canada for the first time when I worked with promoter John McQuade. Years before, I had missed out on the whole Canadian scene with The White Heather Group simply because they hadn't known how to promote me over there so now it was my turn to give it a go and see if I could crack a new market.

On the first tour, we didn't do too badly for a complete unknown and we managed to break even. On our next tour of Canada, my guitarist, Owen, came to be known as the coo's tail as he always arrived last. Cars would come to collect and drive us to the next venue and I'd round the band up only to discover that Owen was missing as usual. I'd go and knock on his door and, nine times out of ten, he would be having a bath, smoking away without a care in the world. Not only that, he'd have his false teeth and his socks in the bath water beside him – it was quite a sight.

I loved everything about Canada, from the people to the countryside, the cities and the venues. In Toronto, we played places like Massey Hall and Hamilton Place, which had a speaker underneath every member of the audience's seat. It also allowed me to catch up with my brother Andy who flew down from Vancouver with his wife Cathie to meet me. I found it funny that it actually took them longer to fly from Vancouver to Toronto than it did for me to fly there from Prestwick – it just shows you what a vast country it is.

John McQuade had, in fact, helped to promote The White Heather Group when they had gone to Canada without me. They were basically just bringing a taste of Scottish music to the Canadian audiences so it had been an easy enough job to promote them but it was a different kettle of fish promoting my show as they didn't quite know what category I fell in to. It kind of helped that my song, 'Scotland, We Love You', was a hit in the Canadian charts at the time but that also meant that many people were turning up expecting to see a Scottish entertainer perform only Scottish songs. They'd get quite a surprise when I'd walk onstage in a white catsuit with rhinestones and thistles on it.

Because we knew the crowd were confused about what they were getting, the first show was a real learning process and the whole band had to think on its feet. After you've been in entertainment for so long, you can tell within five minutes what kind of songs a crowd want. So I started giving them old classics like 'Loch Lomond' and 'Amazing Grace', before throwing in a bit of 'The Green, Green Grass of Home' and, as the saying goes, 'Just give me the keys of the theatre, I'll lock up myself.' It was those songs that they really wanted to hear so I had to totally ditch my normal repetoire.

But this new lease of life had come after my heart attack and I figured, at this stage in my life, I could tackle any new challenge.

25

OUR HOTEL DISASTER

After my heart attack, I did make one terrible mistake that eventually saw us having to quit our huge house. Actually, we moved for a couple of reasons, one being that there was only Shirley and me left and it was like having a mansion for two people. Also, Shirley will not have anybody clean her house for her as she hasn't found anyone who can do it as well as she can. And, similarly, I can't find anyone to do the garden the way I want it done. So that was one good reason to downsize and the other very legitimate reason was that I lost a substantial sum of money on the Anfield Hotel in Ayr which I bought in 1994.

We had been running a pub in Irvine called the Harbour Lights. I had bought some flats to rent out up in Gleneagles during the early 90s but really the only people who ever stayed in them were our friends. At that time my son, Gary, was working on the rigs in the North Sea. This work always left Shirley with her heart in her mouth every time he went away so we decided to sell the flats and open a pub for Gary to run instead. He made a great job of it and it was a very successful business. So, as a progression from that, we started thinking about our retirement and thought it would be good to buy a hotel and one came on sale literally 400 yards from the front door of our house.

When you buy any licensed premises, knowing the annual turnover is extremely important and we had to study the hotel's accounts very closely. But, about six months after we bought the place, we realised the figures we were told by the seller didn't match anything near what we were making – so there was either something wrong with his books or ours. As Shirley meticulously looked after that side of things for us, I doubted we were in the wrong. To put it simply, we weren't making enough money. To Shirley's credit, she had been the first to flag it up but I think everyone was still so enthusiastic and excited by the new business that we gave her fears little attention. We spent a lot of money on improvements but still couldn't get the figures up to anything like they were supposed to be. About a year later, someone told me that the person who sold us the place was done for fraud on another business entirely and I believe he spent three months in jail.

So the worst decision I ever made was buying the Anfield and the best was when I sold it. I think a huge part of the problem was where the hotel was. Now, I love Ayr and it has been our home for decades now but it's a very funny place. If I'd opened a hotel in Glasgow, I reckon business would have been a lot healthier. In Ayr, the locals don't like you to get above your station. I think they resented the fact that Shirley and I had our private registration Mercs or BMWs in the driveway and they would go out of their way not to come into our place. Some even told me to my face that they wouldn't come in for that reason. They don't want you to be too successful down here. But, in saying that, with the exception of Perthshire, I wouldn't stay anywhere else in Scotland.

So, as soon as I got a reasonable offer, we sold the hotel, incurring a loss of quarter of a million pounds over the three years we owned it. We had to sell the Harbour Lights too. That was actually the first to go as there's never any problem selling a good pub. We had taken a big financial blow and so we decided to stick to what I know – singing. After my heart trouble, I had neglected that side of things to concentrate on the pub and hotel in anticipation of having an easier, more comfortable life in later years but I should have never have turned my back on the entertainment business.

I also had to give up the hotel as I was getting in to more fights there than Benny Lynch! Guys would come in off the street to fight with me. It was bizarre. It was as if they saw my car outside and thought, 'That Sydney Devine thinks he's really something about these parts – I'm going in to fight him.' What makes someone do that? Well, I know what it is – it's jealousy.

One incident even made the headlines when it was reported that an over-eager fan had grabbed me by the testicles. This was complete fabrication as no real fan tries to injure you. What actually happened was a bunch of football hooligans had turned up for a drink but they were barred and I told them they weren't going to be served. Of course, as always, there was one loud-mouthed thug who likes to show off and, egged on by his mates, he grabbed me by the testicles – not an area I normally like being grabbed, especially by a fella. As you can imagine, it was agony and Shirley called the police and we had him charged. We had to do that as the attacks were getting out of hand and you simply can't allow people to come on to your premises and assault you like that and get away with it. I'm sure there's some idiot still walking around Ayr, proud that his claim to fame was that he was once busted for grabbing Sydney Devine's goolies – it's probably the highlight of his sad life.

Don't get me wrong, I met a lot of nice people there, including John Storey, big Hughie and Lambert Dunn – as well as being very good customers, these three are exceptionally good people too – but I was glad to get away from the cretins who would come in just to try and wind me up. I wasn't used to nonsense like that.

So I was quarter of a million down, which is a lot of songs, but, although the bank balance had taken a walloping, contrary to what many may have thought, I wasn't broke. I wasn't happy either, mind you. But, then, it's funny how, in this business or in life in general, one door closes and another one opens.

Dougie Stevenson, who's the steel guitarist in my band, had formed a company called Scot Disc with Bill Garden from Kilsyth and I had done a few records for them. One day, Dougie called and said, 'Sydney, I think the next big thing is going to be line dancing – I think you should do a line-dancing album.' I disagreed and told him that the whole line-dancing thing had come and gone in the early 90s but he was most insistent. He said there were still hundreds of line-dancing clubs all over the country and we should give it a bash. So, in 1996, we hired the Old Fruit Market in Glasgow, bought new costumes, rehearsed until we got all the dances right, got an audience in and then recorded and videotaped the show. The fortnight before Christmas, the line-dancing album was outselling Oasis in HMV in Glasgow – I think it did something like 50,000 copies in total. It was a massive seller as no one had ever put together a good line-dancing video before, with popular songs that people could follow easily.

We soon released a sequel, *Line Dance Party 2* and that did almost as well so, thanks to Dougie and the thousands of line-dancing fanatics out there, I was back on an even keel. That's what I love about this game – you never know what's around the corner. But I learned a valuable lesson – in addition to staying clear of the hotel business – and that was that you should never say never and, when someone asks you to do a job, you should do it.

In 2005, I finished another kind of album that I never thought I'd be capable of doing – swing. It's not out-and-out swing as it has more of a dance tempo like the old Victor Silvester songs – so, instead of songs like 'Come Fly with Me', it leans more towards the 'Embrace Me' type of song. People think of me as a country singer and as a rock 'n' roller but maybe now, when they hear my swing album, they'll be calling me the Scottish Sinatra!

It's great to still be going into a studio with Tommy after all these years. I remember when we used to work in London for Phonogram in the 70s and would go for these massive liquid lunches. One time, after a particularly long lunch – five hours long to be precise – we returned to Chappells recording studio. We got in the lift and the bloody thing broke down and alarm bells started going off everywhere. There were maybe about another five people in this lift, including a couple of girls. One of them began to panic and started screaming her head off – believe me, there can't be many things worse than being stuck in a broken-down lift with a woman screaming. So, I turned to Tommy and said, 'Right, there's only one thing to do here – if we're going to die, we may as well enjoy ourselves.' We both winked at each other and promptly dropped our trousers. I thought having a laugh would calm this girl down but it had the opposite effect and caused the other girl to start screaming too because she thought that, as well as being trapped in a lift, she was in the presence of a couple of perverts. As luck would have it, the lift starting moving again and Tommy and I were glad to pull our trousers up and slink off.

26

MY WORK FOR CHARIDEE

In 1994, I was doing a garden fête down in Greenock for a man called Sir Ross Belch who had a lot of influence in Upper Clyde shipbuilding. He had a big house called Alt-na-Craig in Port Glasgow and every year he would open it up to the public. He'd invite various entertainers, like Nicholas Parsons, and there would be stalls and play areas for the kids. Of course, the year I was invited, it would have to be bucketing down with rain. But I got through it, sang a couple of songs with a jazz band, had a good time and even did a video of the event. I think because I had soldiered on and managed to lift everyone's spirits, I instantly hit it off with Sir Ross and we became firm friends. After the 1994 fête, he invited me back the following year and I would stay in touch with Sir Ross right up to the day he died in April 1999.

One day, out of the blue, I got a call from a lady called Pat Yuill. Pat was working for Marie Curie Cancer Care and she said she knew Sir Ross who had recommended that she give me a call. Pat explained that they were opening a Marie Curie shop in Port Glasgow and they would love it if I'd come along to help launch it. I would just be asked to say a few words about Marie Curie, cut the tape and that was to be it so, of course, I said yes.

I arrived in Port Glasgow at 11 o'clock and I couldn't believe my eyes. The street was mobbed – just for the opening of this wee charity shop. I thought, 'I can't just open up the shop, say a few words and go away.' So I grabbed a stool, got on top of it and sang 'Tiny Bubbles' and 'Maggie'. By this time, police motorbikes had arrived because the crowd was now spilling out on to the road and blocking the traffic. I'd brought some photos with me and, after I'd finished singing, I went into this tiny wee shop and I started signing the photos and selling them at 50p a throw. The money from the sale of the photos went to the charity and, in addition to that, they made over seventy quid from one donation can alone.

The *Greenock Telegraph* covered the event and ran a front-page story with the headline 'Traffic Stopped for Sydney'. After the opening of the Port Glasgow shop, Pat said, 'This is amazing Sydney! What's your fee?' I looked at her as if she had two heads. I said, 'It's for Marie Curie – there is no fee.' I was later gobsmacked to hear that many so-called celebrities charge small fortunes for doing charity work. How sick can you get? Surely, when you're asked to help out with something as worthwhile as Marie Curie, the last thing you should do is think of lining your own pockets? Since Port Glasgow, I think I've opened something like twenty-four or twenty-five Marie Curie shops. I've been as far as Aberdeen, Arbroath and Stranraer for them and I don't even charge for my petrol. As far as I'm concerned, I'm honoured that they ask me and I'm just glad that they get such great turnouts for the openings. I only wish more people in my position would get involved and do something to help out because very few families escape the curse of cancer. It's also something I enjoy doing as there aren't too many other ways of giving something back.

27

OUR SPANISH NIGHTMARE

Now, our neighbour in Ayr is Billy Dickson. Billy was an international footballer who played for Kilmarnock and Ayr as well as Scotland and he's some man for the horses. He often comes over to my house to have a beer and watch some football. One day, while we were watching a game, he told me that he and his wife, Linda, had got last-minute flights for about £110 return to Spain. He then asked if The Duchess – which is what he always calls Shirley – and I fancied coming along. Billy had an apartment where we could stay so it would only be a matter of paying for the flights. But, for a couple of reasons, Shirley wasn't keen on the idea. One was the fact that the suggestion we join the Dicksons had been made on a Saturday and the plane left the very next day from Newcastle. But the other reason was that we had vowed never to return after our youngest son, Scot, had been involved in a near-fatal accident there in 1975.

Back then, my brother John and I had met this guy called Tom Howie. Tom owned and ran a couple of frozen food businesses called Howie's of Dunlop and Kyle County. I'd done a few favours for him over the years, including opening gala days and that sort of thing, so, in the mid 70s, as a thank-you, he gave me use of his place in Torra Blanca in Spain rent free. We'd gone over with my brother Geordie and his family and basically had the run of this huge villa for two weeks. One day, everyone decided to go out but I opted to stay by the pool with Scot. As was typical with a lot of Spanish pools then, the pool was around ten-feet deep from one end to the other – there was no shallow end. So I was sitting sunbathing by the pool when I heard a splash. I looked up and spotted the armbands Scot had been using – but there was no sign of Scot. I jumped out of my lounger and rushed over to the pool to see my worst nightmare – my son was lying motionless at the bottom of the pool.

I dived down, grabbed him by the wrist and dragged him out and on to the side of the pool. It had only been a matter of seconds – thirty at the most – from the time I heard the splash to the moment I got him out of the water but Scot wasn't breathing. Although my heart was in my mouth, luckily I didn't panic and I set about squeezing the water out of his lungs. There was an awful moment when I was pumping his chest and water was gushing out of his mouth and nose but there were still no signs of life. Then, suddenly, Scot started spluttering and coughing and, when he started crying, I knew I had him back – those seconds, when I was trying to revive him but nothing appeared to be doing any good, seemed the longest of my life. So I just sat there and held on to his little body and refused to let him go. I had almost lost my son in that ridiculously deep swimming pool. I know Shirley would have never forgiven me if our younger son had drowned on my watch.

Scot suffered ill health for around six months after that horrific incident – he just wasn't right. As well as worrying about his health, I had a recurring nightmare in which I saw myself being unable to pull him from the pool in time and I kept beating myself up about what had happened. What if I had fallen asleep? What if I hadn't heard the splash? What if I hadn't noticed his armbands as quickly as I did? God knows what would have happened. So, because of our awful memories, we basically never went back to Spain for over twenty years – until Billy convinced us to join him and his wife on this cheap holiday.

While we were watching that football game on the TV, we checked the price of the flights again on Teletext and the cost of the tickets had dropped to just £78. So, after some wine and a little persuasion from Billy, we decided it was about time we went back and exorcised our demons.

But, shortly after arriving, we wished we'd never agreed to go. We were driving up a hill from the airport to get to Billy's apartment when all those dark memories came flooding back. I realised we were in exactly the same area as the one where we had so nearly lost Scot. I couldn't believe how raw the emotions still felt. Billy's place must have been only quarter of a mile from the villa where we had stayed all those years ago and I could see the look of horror creep over Shirley's face as well – she, too, simply couldn't believe we had returned to somewhere that was so near the scene of the accident.

We felt very unsettled for the first day or so but, fortunately, we had our grandson, Ryan, with us and looking after him helped to keep our minds from dwelling on the horror of the last time we'd been to Spain. We spent most of the time down the beach – staying well clear of any pools. Eventually, we began to relax and we ended up having a really good time. We were there in October and the weather was wonderful. And there were festivals during which the Spaniards would come out in all their finery, riding their magnificent horses. Even the kids were dressed in beautiful Spanish costumes. Because we were in the middle of all these festivities, it actually turned into one of the best week's holiday we'd ever had – and, not only did we have a fabulous time in Spain, we were finally able to face a really dreadful event from the past that had, in our minds, come to be associated with that country.

In fact, we had fallen in love with Spain and we ended up travelling back and forth a few times. The location was perfect as we were only two hours from Cordoba and two hours from Granada and the Sierra Nevada for the skiing in the winter. Every time we went, we were always on the lookout to see if there was anything we fancied buying and we eventually bought a flat on the fifth floor of a complex at the top of Torra Blanca. We spent a lot of money doing it up, adding air conditioning and decorating, but there was one drawback – it only had one bedroom. It was really far too small because, as soon as you buy somewhere, it's only natural that your family will want to join you.

So, in 2002, we bought a place that was being built on a golf course. I don't want to seem like I'm boasting so I won't – suffice to say, it's big enough to have the family come for visits. But, I reckon, after over fifty years of working hard, it was high time Shirley and I really treated ourselves. Although we go over to Spain several times a year, I would never leave Scotland permanently. But I have to admit it's becoming increasingly difficult to justify having our two homes. The cost of living in the UK – everything from petrol and food, to income tax and council tax – is exceptionally high. How ordinary people with an average wage can afford to stay in Scotland now is beyond me.

At one point in the early 80s, I was quite political and I supported the Conservatives. This was because, in the 70s when Harold Wilson's government was in power, I was being taxed 83p for every pound I earned, which was crazy. That was why the likes of Sean Connery left the country, which is fair enough, but I don't think knighthoods should go to people who don't pay any tax. That really gets up my nose! I was never an active Conservative and I eventually gave up on all of the politicians because I realised that it really didn't matter which party was in power – they were all the same.

I still have strong views and, most of all, I know what's fair and what's not fair. For example, I don't think pensioners over sixty-five should have to pay council tax – no matter how much money they have. I know the council tax is for local services but, by the time they reach that age, they will have been paying taxes for around fifty years. Then, once they have retired and are earning less, they still have to keep paying them until the day they die. Folk over the age of seventy-five get a free TV licence but big wow! How many people, especially men, live to see their seventy-fifth birthday?

I know I've been fortunate to have been able to make a comfortable living over the years but, even at the age of sixty-five, I still work – maybe not as much as I used to but I still do what I can.

OK, I'll come down from my soapbox! I think it's a fair comment to say that, years after what could have been a tragedy, that trip to Spain has improved our lives no end and I'll always be grateful to Billy for convincing us to go back.

28

MIGHTY CRAIC

Now, one of the best things about being out on tour – apart from the performances, of course – is the craic with the band. Because you spend so much time with each other and are practically living out of one another's pockets, having a laugh is one of the best ways of relieving any tension or even boredom as there's nothing more boring than the long-distance travelling between gigs. The laughs I've had on tour are what I enjoyed the most about being on the road and I will always cherish the memories of the fun times we had.

The smallest, stupidest things could crack us up for days on end. For example, I was in Norwich in 1982 and, after the gig, we were all in the hotel for a dram or two to help us come down from the performance – which was something we always did. Our drummer, John O'Neil, had gone to try to get hold of the manager for some reason – probably to do with getting some more booze for the band. When he opened the door to the manager's office, he was confronted by a massive, snarling German shepherd. It was one of those big aggressive dogs that would tear your head off as soon as look at you. It obviously gave John quite a scare and all we could hear was him shouting at the hotel manager the immortal phrase, 'See that dog of yours – it's a f***ing animal!'

Another time in the same city, Shirley and I were celebrating our twenty-fifth wedding anniversary. She'd come down to join me but, as I was in the middle of the tour, I had completely forgotten what date it was – something no husband is ever allowed to forget. To make matters worse, it was a Sunday so the chances of buying a big bouquet of flowers were greatly reduced. I explained the situation to Dougie Stevenson who has worked with me for thirty-two years now – firstly, as my steel guitarist and, latterly, as my recording manager. I told him the predicament I was in and asked if there was any way he could help me. Dougie was as laid back as ever and told me not to worry about a thing and just to leave it with him. That night, Dougie came into the theatre with the most incredible flower arrangement I have ever seen in my life – and Shirley was blown away by them and my thoughtfulness! The flowers really were spectacular and I was hugely impressed by how Dougie had managed to save the day for me. After the show, it was back to the hotel for a drink as usual and it was then that I noticed some very similar flower arrangements around the foyer. But I thought no more about it – Shirley was happy and that was all that mattered.

The next morning, we were checking out and as I went to settle the bill, Shirley placed her bouquet of flowers on the reception desk. The woman on reception took the flowers and put them behind the desk. Shirley said, 'Err, excuse me, those are my flowers.' The receptionist replied, 'Actually, I think they're the hotel's flowers, madam.' Well, this was like a red rag to a bull and Shirley said firmly, 'No, they're mine – my husband bought them for me for our anniversary.' Shirley then reached over the counter, grabbed the flowers and marched out. Later, I told Dougie what had happened and he said, 'Well, you asked for flowers and I got you some – you never asked where I got them from.'

We would also keep pranks and running jokes going for days, sometimes weeks on end. We were in Oban in 1984 and in the cast that time was the singer, Anne Williamson, and the late Gary Dennis, who was a tremendous comedian from Edinburgh. While we were travelling there on our tour bus, I turned round and said to our lead guitarist, Owen Knox, in front of everyone, 'You turn the volume down tonight – don't be playing as loud as last night.' Owen picked up the bait and told me to mind my own business. He said he would play at whatever volume he felt like playing because, as the lead guitarist, that was his prerogative.

You could cut the atmosphere with a knife for the rest of the journey as Owen and I pretended to be seething with each other and the rest of the cast sat in silence. Not content with that, when we arrived at the venue, we decided to heat up the situation with the aid of a joke blood capsule. Half an hour before the show, Owen and I started arguing again and he swung a punch at me that seemed to send me sprawling on the floor. Everyone rushed over and looked at me lying there motionless, with 'blood' streaming from my mouth. Gary Dennis bent down beside me and it took him an age to bring me round and shuffle me off to my dressing room. By this point, everyone was panicking – the top of the bill had a bloody mouth and was concussed and there was less than half an hour before the curtain was due to go up.

As well as doing his comedy routine, Gary was to be compèring that night so Owen pulled Gary aside and told him, 'Before the start of the show, make sure you tell the crowd that the band's records are available to buy at the end of the night.' Gary was rushing around like a headless chicken and, before the curtain went up, he came into my dressing room to check on how I was feeling. I put on an act and told him I was feeling terrible and then I said, 'By the way, Gary, don't mention that bastard's records are for sale.' By this time, Gary was looking like a rabbit caught in the headlamps. I then told Gary I would be fit enough to go onstage but I said I would need to wash my hair and asked Gary if he could borrow a hairdryer from someone in the band. Overhearing this, Owen picked up an electric fire and told Gary, 'This is good enough for the shithead.'

Unfortunately, we were a bit too convincing as not only did Gary go to the grave believing that Owen and I hated each other's guts but the local newspaper actually ran a report on our behind-the-scenes bust-up. Someone at the venue must have tipped off a reporter about how we couldn't bear to be in the same room together.

But one time, in Campbeltown, we took our little in-jokes too far. I had travelled there with *The Andy Stewart Show* and was on the bill with Dixie Ingram who, like Andy at that time, was also a regular on telly. We were on the bus and we'd got about halfway there when Dixie started saying things like, 'You know, Sydney, you cannae bloody sing nothing anyway' and 'Sydney, when it comes down to it, you're really just a tuppence ha'penny singer.' I acted as though I was really wounded and I replied, 'Aye, well, Dixie, I just try to do my best.'

Dixie kept this up all the way until we got into the bar at The Royal Hotel in Campbeltown where there were some people waiting for autographs. So I piped up again, 'OK, Dixie, everyone's entitled to their opinion so I hear you and I know I'm not the greatest singer but can you just leave it there? I'm not as lucky as you to be on the telly and I'm just trying to earn a living.' There was silence in the bar as the locals realised they were in the middle of an explosive situation here. Dixie put his glass down and, as loud as you like, he said, 'Not only are you not the greatest singer, you're an unlucky-looking bastard as well. Are you sure your mother married your father?' Just then, some big bloke who had been sitting in the corner sprang up, bolted across the room and landed a cracking right hook on Dixie's jaw, knocking him on his arse.

Shortly after that incident, we made a pact that, if we were going to carry on like that again, we'd only ever do it in private in case someone actually got their jaw broken. But, I must admit, I was pretty chuffed that a fan had been so keen to spring to my defence in such dramatic fashion.

However, even that didn't stop us larking around entirely. I returned to The Royal Hotel in 1987 when BBC TV were making a documentary about my career. We had been filming all day with a brilliant producer called Sean Hardie, who had also made *Not the Nine O'Clock News*. At night, we were gathered in the bar when I asked everyone if they had ever heard of the ghost of Campbeltown's Royal Hotel. Most people, like my drummer John O'Neil, were saying things like, 'Aye, that'll be right, Sydney!' But I continued, saying, 'No, I'm telling you, I've been coming here for years and I've heard several guests mention it. Ask the staff – most of them have seen something. This place really is haunted.'

What I'd told them certainly seemed to do the trick as John then said, 'I hate the room I'm in anyway – it's freaky! There's kids' cots kept in there and everything.' I told him 'Ah, well, actually it was a baby that died in this hotel and, seemingly, the ghost that's been seen is the grieving mother, going in and out of the rooms looking for her bairn.' I'd obviously got to John at this point because he shouted out, 'Don't tell me lies – don't say that!' I apologised, said I was going to bed and told John not to be late as we started filming early doors. But, instead of going off to my bed, I got the night porter to open John's door for me – he knew we were pals – and I hid under his bed.

All the time I was lying under there, I was killing myself laughing – I'd taken a right attack of the giggles. But, about five minutes later, I heard John coming up the stairs to his room and I managed to stifle my laughter. He came in, switched the light on and had just sat down on his bed to take his trousers off when I grabbed his ankles. I think his screams could have been heard in Ayrshire. He ran from that room, shrieking all the way down the corridor, and woke up the whole hotel. It was the funniest thing I've ever seen in my life and I just couldn't get out from under that bed for laughing. Sometimes there are things you shouldn't do to people and that was probably one of them because John could have easily died of a heart attack that night.

Theatrical digs were also places where we had great laughs. I'll never forget Nanny Martin's at 39 Back Wynd in Aberdeen. Old Nanny had deer heads on the staircase and no running water – plenty of deer heads but you couldn't get near a tap – so you had to wait until you got to the theatre before you could have a wash. The room I stayed in was nicknamed The Covered Wagon by Jack Milroy as that's exactly what it looked like – a wagon from a western film. There was a basin with a ewer – a big porcelain jug – and they used to bring you up some hot water in the morning so you could wash your face and have a shave although, as I said, it was a lot easier if you just waited until you were in the venue.

Old Nanny had a brother called Leo who rarely ventured from his tiny, dank room and, when he did, it was obvious he was wearing boot polish on his head in a vain attempt to disguise his baldness. But, between them, they had run their digs for theatre folk all their lives. Everyone had stayed at Nanny Martin's – Jack Milroy actually stayed in Nanny's guest house the night before his wedding. Nanny might have had antiquated bathroom facilities but what she lacked in the running water department she more than made up for with her roast potatoes. Nanny made the best roast potatoes I've ever tasted and I haven't had roast potatoes like them since. Those delicious tatties made up for everything else as far as I was concerned!

29

MY UNFALTERING FANS

I have never been one to take my fans for granted and I'm so grateful to my die-hard supporters who turn out in numbers that never cease to amaze me. At one point, there were even bus tours taking fans past my home in Ayr! After taking tourists down to the land of Rabbie Burns, as a little extra outing, the bus companies would then drive up my road, which was fairly near Burns' Cottage, and you would be able to hear them announce over their tannoy, 'And here is the palatial home of Sydney Devine.' Although I didn't mind, I think it caught Shirley off guard once or twice when she was sunbathing by our pool and, all of a sudden, loads of camera flashbulbs started going off.

I may not receive anywhere near that sort of level of attention these days but my fans are still out there. I have a hardcore group of them who come to every gig I do. There's Linley Park from Aberdeen. She has been a fan for the best part of forty years and, recently, she sent me a magnificent scrapbook charting all the years she has been following me. Then there's the secretary of my fan club, Pat Munro, Lily Paterson, Christine Paterson and Catherine McGuigan who are all stalwarts. Another is Veronica Simms from Kent. She comes up from England with her husband George to see my shows at The Pavilion. Other well-travelled members of the audience are Jackie Pantry from Leeds and John Dodds from Blythe in Northumberland. And a special mention must go to Peter McMahon of the Easterhouse Handicap Club.

I'm on first name terms with most of the regulars in the audience at The Pavilion these days and it almost feels like being back in the old days at the Finlayson Arms where I got to know all of the crowd and every performance was like one big party. That's the way it is now and I wouldn't have it any other way.

For the last twenty years at the Pavilion Theatre, I have always invited fans to my dressing room, after the show finishes, so that I can give them my autograph. Because I normally do my gigs at The Pavilion later in the year, I don't like to have people standing waiting for me to sign their programmes or whatever out in the cold. But there's one lady, Jenny Wardrop, and her son, Thomas, who would stand outside in the snow and the pouring rain just to meet me. They have always given me presents for the grandchildren and Christmas gifts for Shirley and they have continued to do so to this very day. Now, *that's* what I call dedication.

Tam Cowan has his own BBC TV football show called *Offside* and, with Stuart Cosgrove, he also presents a light-hearted look at Scottish football on the BBC Radio Scotland programme, *Off the Ball*. Well, I only discovered quite recently that he and his mother have been coming to see me at The Pavilion for the last twenty years. I think Tam is something of a frustrated stage performer himself. Although he is a past master of the piss-take on radio and TV, he's never had a pop at me – even though he's had me on his football TV show as I used to be a big Ayr United supporter.

I would go along every second week to Somerset Park, pay my money like everyone else and take my place in the stand. But eventually my heart just couldn't take it any more! I think that was maybe one of the reasons I had a heart attack. You don't mind getting beaten sometimes but, when you're getting beaten week in, week out, that's just torture. I remember the great days of Ayr when they had players like Spud Murphy, Alan Ingram, Alex Mcanespie and people like that. Then they had a great team and even Rangers and Celtic found it very, very difficult to come to Somerset Park and go away with the points. And they played some really good football in those days too.

But back to Tam – it seems that, on one of his first dates with his girlfriend, Liz Steele, he took her to one of my concerts. It couldn't have put her off as she ended up marrying him!

30

LOGAN'S RUN

In 1998, the Scottish tycoon, John Boyle, decided to launch a company called Direct Cruises. John owns Motherwell Football Club and he also ran the very successful Direct Holidays empire which was what led to him branching out into the cruise holiday market. The idea was that a cruise ship would sail from Greenock and take passengers sailing around the Mediterranean. It seemed like the project couldn't fail but, unfortunately, it got off to a disastrous start when the ship was beset with problems and John ended up having to pay out a staggering £10 million in compensation after the first season – but, wait a minute, I'm getting ahead of myself.

John kindly asked Shirley and me to go on the maiden voyage but there were so many problems with the ship and the delays were so long that we ended up having to leave from Liverpool. We were disappointed not to be sailing from Greenock but we understood that these things happen. So we travelled down to Merseyside and there we were to be joined by members of the cabaret who included the singer, Rose Marie, and the impressionist, Faith Brown.

You know how, when one thing goes wrong, everything starts to go wrong? Well, this was one of those situations. These two 'stars' turned up with their entourages – and I do mean entourages – and began demanding a suite for this one and a suite for that one. Because all the berths on the ship

197

were booked, there was no way the ship could accommodate them so all the cabaret turns just turned around and walked off. Having already struggled with the ship's waterlogged cabins, poor John Boyle was now faced with the prospect of having no cabaret for the maiden voyage of his new business venture.

As if things weren't bad enough already, everyone then started complaining. Now I can understand that, if you've spent good money, you should be offered first-class service but, as far as we were concerned, we had no complaints at all. The food was excellent, the rooms we had were luxurious and the locations were all fabulous.

Onboard with us was Jimmy Logan and his fourth wife, Angela – not the same wife I had a crush on all those years ago and who had taught me to dance like Elvis Presley. Now, believe it or not, despite us both having been in the business for decades, Jimmy and I had never met but, on that cruise ship, we instantly hit it off and became great friends.

One of the best times we had was when we took a day trip to Casablanca with Jimmy. Angela wasn't feeling well so she stayed behind. When Jimmy saw some camels, he tried to exchange them for Shirley. He told the herder that, for the exchange to take place, he wanted three camels because Shirley was so voluptuous! We eventually arrived at the place that was supposed to be Rick's American Bar – the one that Humphrey Bogart's Rick Blaine ran in the film *Casablanca* – and Jimmy sat down at the piano and started playing 'You Must Remember This'. He was a lovely pianist and, before you knew it, he was in full flow. Next he was telling the crowd gags and one that I remember goes like this:

A guy goes into a bar and says to the barman, 'If I show you something you've never seen in your life before, will you give me a drink for nothing?' The barman says, 'Look, I've been in this game for forty-odd years so you can't surprise me – I've seen the whole lot.' So the guy goes into his pocket and pulls out a miniature man and out of his other pocket he pulls out a mini grand piano and the wee man sits down and plays the piano, note perfect. The barman says, 'You're right! I have never seen anything like that in my life before!' So he gives the guy a large brandy and a pint of lager. The barman then asks, 'How did you get hold of him?' The guy says, 'Well, I was standing at the corner of Sauchiehall Street one day and this old woman couldn't get across the road so I took her hand and walked her to the other side as the traffic was that busy. The old woman said, "I'm a witch and I can grant you one wish for your kindness." Now, I don't know if it was the noise of the traffic or if she was hard of hearing but I finished up with this 12-inch pianist!'

He had the crowd roaring with laughter. But that was Jimmy. He could entertain them anywhere – including Casablanca, as it turned out.

After we left Casablanca, Jimmy told me that he was going to do a wee spot of cabaret as the ship's entertainment manager, Clark Stewart, had asked him to do a turn. As there was no band on board, I said, 'But what are you going to do for music?' It turned out that Jimmy had brought a mini-disc player with him along with some music and even a kilt too just in case such an occasion arose – as I said, he could perform anywhere. I said, 'Thanks very much, Jimmy, you've come prepared to do a turn and here I am with nothing – you've made me feel like a right idiot! We're the only two guests here and you'll be earning your keep and I won't.'

So I spoke to John Boyle and said, 'Look, I'd like to help you but there's no way I can go on and do an hour-and-a-half spot without my band.' And, in a matter-of-fact way John said, 'That's no problem – we'll just fly your band over.' Anyway, after several frantic phone calls, he was absolutely true to his word. He flew the full band out from Glasgow to Lisbon, first class, and we did a couple of spots for him on the ship. They were great gigs although we performed in rough seas and the hardest part was trying to keep your feet. But it helped get John out the manure a little and it was the very least we could do.

That whole trip ended up costing John dear but he was always a true gent and an honest businessman who made sure everyone was compensated for their troubles and you can't fault the man for that. But, undoubtedly, the best part for us was meeting Jimmy. We became great pals and remained so right up to his death in 2001. I even performed at his benefit concert a couple of months before he died. I'm just sad that I only got to know him for those three short years as it felt like we'd been friends for life. Shirley and I still miss him.

31

THE BUBBLE THAT WON'T BURST

Now, a book about my life would be incomplete without mentioning my three most famous songs – 'Tiny Bubbles', 'Maggie' and 'The Answer to Everything'.

'Tiny Bubbles' came about in the 60s while I was on my way to Australia with *The Andy Stewart Show* and we stopped over in Hawaii to break the journey. It had been a hell of a flight as we'd gone from Glasgow to London, London to Paris, Paris to New York and New York to Boston before flying from Boston to Honolulu, where we were to spend three days on a sort of mini break before our tour began.

One night, we went along to a venue called the Polynesian Palace. We'd come to watch a local singer called Don Ho, who was the Elvis Presley of Hawaii, and to down a few Mai Tais – the local firewater. Don had had a big hit there with 'Tiny Bubbles' but this was the first time in my life I'd ever heard it. I immediately loved it and thought what a catchy wee song it was. The whole audience loved it too and they were all singing along and I was soon joining in. I bought Don's album and took it with me to learn the song but the first opportunity I had to sing it was on the tour of South Africa in 1969. It turned out to be a huge crowd favourite and I knew I was on to something. Now, everyone thinks of it as my song and no one even mentions that it was Don Ho who originally sang it. The song was written by Leon Pober and I reckon his royalties from the sales of my version had him saying a little prayer every night – something along the lines of 'God bless Sydney Devine!'

I must have performed it over a thousand times in the last thirty-odd years but I never get sick of it. I'm not one of these artists who ends up resenting their old songs – no way. In fact, I wish I had another 100 just like it. And, just as I also never tire of singing it, the audiences never tire of hearing it. Put it this way, if I didn't do 'Tiny Bubbles' onstage I'd get the jail.

It's the same with 'Maggie'. That came about when I was in The White Heather Group and there was this old fella in the group called Jimmy Reid. We used to call him Maggie Reid as his big number was 'Maggie' and each and every time he performed it, he would cry real tears. Jimmy always sang it in a traditional manner, with a very slow beat. I thought it was a nice song but I reckoned it could do with being slightly faster and with a bit of rhythm behind it. Years later, when I was solo, I'd perform it just like that.

'The Answer to Everything' was actually the B-side of Del Shannon's 'Runaway' and it was written by the great Burt Bacharach. I just instantly liked it so I decided to record it. Again, it's one I have to do or the fans would call the polis.

I love the fact that the crowd only have to hear the first few bars of any of these tracks and they go bananas. I may not have written these wonderful tracks but they have become my babies and I will sing them as long as I have a breath in my body.

32

MEETING HER MAJESTY

When I arrived at Buckingham Palace the gods had certainly decided to rain on my parade as it was chucking it down. I was there in my kilt, Shirley was in a beautiful dress, my daughter wore a lovely flowery number and my son Gary had on a smart suit – and we were all gradually getting wetter and wetter as we only had one umbrella between the four of us.

Once we got inside the palace, the courtiers asked various things. I think I must have been asked my name about twenty times before I was allowed anywhere near the Queen. We were taken into the Portrait Gallery where we were given a refreshment. There was nothing alcoholic – only orange juice and water were on offer. A little pin was attached to my lapel to make it easier for the Queen to put the medal on. Then someone came in and instructed everyone how to address the Queen and to say 'ma'am' – as in spam – and not 'marem' – as in harm. They also show you how to take your bow and tell you that, when the Queen grabs your hand you know your time with Her Majesty is at an end and she will be moving on to the next person.

I was about twenty-sixth in line and, by the time she got to the person two before me, I could see Shirley and my son Gary telling me to adjust my tie. But, by that point, my tie was the least of my worries as my nerves were starting to get the better of me and my legs were shaking – I just couldn't stop them. It was quite obvious because, as Shirley remarked afterwards, she was a fair distance away and even she could see my kilt shaking. About fifteen seconds before I actually got to speak to the Queen, I started thinking, 'God Almighty, here's this guy from the village of Bellside who's ended up Buckingham Palace.' When I thought of the unbelievable journey I'd been on to get to this point in my life, I was overwhelmed with emotion.

After the Queen and I exchanged some words, only a few of which I can remember, she did actually grab my hand and push me away. It took me a second to realise what was going on but finally it sunk in – my time with her was over. You have to remember to take one step back when you leave her, bow and then, when you leave the Great Hall, a courtier takes the medal from you and places it in a nice wee box.

I was just so glad I didn't cry in front of her. Afterwards, though, I just couldn't help myself – the floodgates opened and I had a good greet!

I received my MBE on the same day as the telly cook, Jamie Oliver. I said hello to Jamie and then I noticed what he was wearing. Let's just say I was *not* impressed by his dress sense – he wasn't wearing a tie and hadn't shaved. He must have thought he was so cool but I just thought he was an idiot. If it had been up to me, he wouldn't have been allowed in there. They go to great pains to tell you beforehand what the dress code is. For men, it's morning suits or military uniforms although national dress is permitted so Scotsmen may wear kilts. So I thought it was an absolute disgrace for someone to turn up to be presented to the Queen looking as if they'd been dragged through a hedge backwards.

I've been in the business long enough to know what he was up to – it was for publicity. That boy just loves the focus of the world being on him no matter what he's doing. His dishevelled, couldn't-care-less appearance served its purpose because he got his name and his photograph in all the papers and I suppose that's all he wanted.

I wouldn't have been awarded the MBE in the first place if it hadn't been for my devout fans and friends Liz and Harry Stevenson. They've been supporters for a long, long time. Liz kept saying to me, 'It's about time you were recognised.' I would always say, 'Aye, well, maybe one of these days, Liz.' Anyway, lo and behold, when I did receive my MBE, she revealed that she was the one who had written to Tony Blair and really pushed for me to be recognised. The amount of work she must have done to achieve that is quite unbelievable but it just sums up my fans. They're a truly unique bunch and loyal to the last.

33

DEVINE FRIENDS

Over the years, many of the people Shirley and I have come to know have made our lives better in so many ways. Top of the list are Bill and Betty Torrance. We have been friends with them for nearly thirty years and they have seen us through the good, the bad and the occasionally ugly moments that life has a habit of throwing at you. Bill also taught me to fly-fish and he has promised that, one of these days, he will take me on a fishing trip to Alaska and pay for everything – including the fishing permits. As Betty would say, 'Dream on!'

We've spent many happy Sunday lunches with Sir Adrian and Lesley Shinwell. Yes, the vintage port was absolutely devine – sorry, I couldn't resist that one.

Dave and Sheena Curlett have also been good drinking buddies. Dave can pour drink like a Spanish barman with a boil under his arm. He never likes to waste seven inches of vodka by adding too much ice or tonic. Oh, happy days – some of which I nearly remember.

Stewart and Marion Gibson have done more than their fair share of dog- and house-watching.

Graham (better known as Sparky) and Margaret Tannock are very nice people but I never did get to hear the end of their story about the ten million Russians fighting the Irish navy.

We look forward to visiting Robert and Nancy Woods and Jessie and Robert Goldie in Florida again.

Our skiing adventures with Stuart and Linda Laing were world class and Stuart is the only person I have met to this day who can ski uphill backwards – that is when he can find his car keys! Their golf game is very good but on the icy slopes – forget it.

Jan Tomasik, ex-manager of The Apollo in Glasgow has indeed been a very excellent friend to the Devines. Many a time he drove all the way down to Ayr from Glasgow to lend support and help when we really needed it. Jan, to you and Rhona, we will always be eternally grateful.

Then there is the Groden family from Newton Mearns – Bernard and Patricia. I opened quite a few Gardens of Wizo for Patricia and they have been Pavilion regulars since I started performing there thirty-one years ago. I recently met them on a flight to Malaga and promised them a game of golf on the Costa del Sol.

Billy Dickson and his wife, Linda the Shirt Ripper, were instrumental in rekindling our love of Spain and they're great neighbours into the bargain – apart from when their customers park their cars across our gate!!!

Iain Gordon, manager of The Pavilion, and I go back a long way – right back to the days when a ukulele was as good as a banjo, unless you were a George Formby impersonator. Iain, to you and all your staff, thanks for thirty-one great years – long may I have the health to continue there.

The St Quivox surgery and Kirkhall surgery in Prestwick have always taken great care of me and my sincere appreciation goes to Dr Willie Roy and his son Dr David Roy, Dr Steven Glen, the late Dr John McConnell, Dr Bob Percival, Dr Anna Smith and Dr Sylvia Woods, a fanatical Man U supporter. Apart from being our doctor for over twenty years, we enjoyed some fabulous times skiing with Sylvia Woods in

Austria and sharing an odd glass of wine here and there. Both Sylvia Woods and Willie Roy have now retired but my best wishes go to them and all the nurses and staff who, over the years, have tried to keep me in tip-top condition.

I may have accidentally missed out some close friends and people I've known over the years so I would just like to make my apologies to those of you I've forgotten – you know, with age, the memory does begin to fail!

Four of my siblings are still alive: the Jean Blade lives in Wishaw; the Lorna Blade lives in Corby; the Danny Boy lives in Hayton, Nottinghamshire, with his wife Rita; and the Andy Boy lives in Vancouver. It's a privilege to be their brother.

My immediate family deserves my heartfelt thanks for lasting the pace and catering to my every whim.

There is no mileage in the saying, 'If at first you don't succeed . . . then CHEAT!' My mentor, Robert Wilson, once told me, 'Whatever you are, be a good one and be nice to the people on the way up as they will all be waiting for you on the way down.'

Since I started topping the bill in 1974, I have been privileged to work with some very fine entertainers, namely: Gary Dennis, Benn Gunn, Eddie Devine, Billy Jeffries, Neil Owen, Clem Dane, Andy Cameron, Dougie Small, Jimmy Nairn, Anne Williamson, Wilma Andrews, Flo Stevens, Kimberley Clarke, Peppa George, Lorraine Summers, Kathleen Kerr, Joe Gordon and Sally Logan, Jock Morgan, the Scottish fiddler, Tom Ferrie from Radio Clyde, Ethna Campbell, Lena Martell, David and Bernadette, the Maclean Sisters, the great John Shearer and Dippy the Duck, Bert Cohen, Helen Randell, Linda Symon, Janey Kirk, Mr Abe, Dean Park, The Fowler Twins, the late, great Lena Zavaroni, Peters and Lee, Lou Grant, Buddy Greco, Alexander Morrison, Jeannie Maxwell and the Glaswegians Jazz Band, tap-dancing Bill Toner and The Honeybirds, Stella Parton, Jeannie Pruet, and Jean Shepeard.

Good supporting acts make the top-of-the-bill's job one hundred times easier. My thanks and appreciation to one and all. And sincere thanks to Ali Bally at Radio Tay, Roy Waller at Radio Norfolk, Robbie Shepherd at BBC Radio Scotland and Angus Simpson at Saga Radio.

And, as they say, last but by no means least, I must pay tribute to Legend, my band of over thirty years, for their fabulous service and the umpteen laughs we've shared along the way. So, to Bill Garden, Dougie Stevenson, John O'Neil, David Irwin, Frankie Hepburn and Owen Knox, mucho gracias, señores.

34

MY CANCER SCARE

In my late teens, my father was bothered with chronic prostate problems. It wasn't so much a pain issue for him – it was just that he was constantly having to go to the toilet. At one point, he was admitted to hospital in Glasgow to have an operation which involved putting a needle down his penis – ouch! I never thought I would inherit this problem from him until, at the end of 2004, I found myself getting up three or four times a night. Sometimes I would just get back into bed and I immediately felt I had to go again but it was more an inconvenience than anything else. Then I discovered that my brother, Danny, who lives in Lincolnshire, had the same problem and my other brother, Andy, in Vancouver also suffered from it. But more worrying was the fact that my brother, Geordie, had died from prostate cancer and my other brother, Hugh, had also died following complications resulting from prostate trouble.

At the start of 2005, I was referred to the urology unit at Ayr Hospital where I met the consultant, Mr Hollins. I had to pass water into a machine that would record the power of my urine flow. Mr Hollins then studied the results and told me that the amount of water I passed should have taken between eighteen and twenty-three seconds to produce but it had taken me a minute and a half. He was quite cheery though and said, 'It would appear, Mr Devine, that you have a bit of a prostate problem down there'. Of course, at my age, they have to keep a close eye on the prostate in case the problem's cancerous.

Because my brother died from prostate cancer then, of course, I was worried about having the same thing. Geordie had actually had an operation to remove the cancer but then, two years later, the cancer went into his bones and killed him. He broke his leg at one point and his bones were so weak they couldn't even stick a pin in them to put him back together. A number of people I've known have died from the same thing – prostate cancer seems to spread to the bones quickly for some reason – so it was only natural that all of this would cross my mind.

They did a battery of tests on me and would stick fingers where the sun don't shine. But, fortunately, my blood tests showed no sign of cancer and they reckoned it was a hardening of the prostate rather than anything more sinister.

I went to Spain for six weeks at the start of 2005 and, when I returned, a Mr Meddings was to carry out the operation to alleviate the problem. I went into Ayr Hospital on a Sunday and was admitted to a ward with a bunch of fellas who were all in for the same thing. I have to say the craic was fantastic and even the nurses said we were the best bunch of patients they'd had in a long time. The operation went without a glitch. Apparently, there had been a growth on my prostate and they had chopped it off with some electronic gizmo. They had to send the growth off for analysis to make sure it wasn't cancerous and, fortunately, I soon got the all-clear.

The day after the op, I had to wander around the ward with a catheter poking out the front of my pyjama trousers and, somewhat embarrassingly, the weight of the tube usually meant that it pulled everything out the front of your bottoms too for all and sundry to see. I was glad to hear I wasn't the only one who suffered from this humiliating problem and one day I heard a cry from one of the other beds, 'Davie, for Christ's sake, your starting handle's hanging out!' I loved that and all the nurses fell about laughing too. But you needed to have a laugh as it helped to lighten the mood and enabled you to keep your dignity. I mean, one day, I was walking up and down the ward for some exercise with the three other patients in the ward, each of us carrying our own bags of urine with us. No wonder we all wanted to be tucked up in bed, with our bags hidden away, when it came to visiting time.

The staff took my catheter out after three days and the first time in the toilet it was literally like passing glass. After that, it became a bit easier but they then scan you with an ultrasound – much like they do with pregnant women – and they can tell how much water has been retained in your bladder. The guy opposite me, Davie, was scanned and told he had 47mm of urine in his bladder so he was getting out. It was my turn next and I had 247mm left. The nurse told me to keep drinking and trying to pass it and she would scan me again. After another couple of hours, the amount of urine retained in my bladder had gone up to 300mm and I couldn't pass anything. However, shortly after that, I was eventually able to pass quite a lot of water and the level was then low enough for them to allow me to go home.

Although I was in a lot of pain, like anyone who's been in hospital, I just couldn't wait to get home. Despite drinking plenty during that first day back at home, by 10 o'clock at night, again I couldn't pass a thing. I went to bed but woke at 12.25 to try and go again – nothing. After another fifteen minutes, I was in the bathroom once more but still not a drop and, by this time, I was in agony. So I phoned the ward and said I was having great difficulty passing water. They told me I'd better come in right away as an emergency case. Shirley is a terrible sleeper as she has restless legs syndrome and she hadn't had a wink of sleep since I went into hospital. The annoying thing was that, this particular night, she was sound asleep and I was reluctant to wake her. She looked so peaceful so I left her alone but, before long, I was on the carpet in agony and had no choice but to waken her.

Poor Shirley had to rush me down to accident and emergency where this lovely little female doctor, who was actually from Cumnock, scanned me and discovered I had over a litre of water in my bladder. They had to get a catheter into me straight away because, with that amount of urine, there's a strong chance your bladder can burst. It's all right having a catheter inserted when you're unconscious in theatre but it's not the most pleasant procedure when you're wide awake and already writhing in agony.

Afterwards, I was taken back up to the same ward again where I was met by the guys. They greeted me with, 'Welcome home – so good you couldn't stay away, eh, Sydney?'

The next morning Mr Meddings came in to do his rounds and was quite surprised to see me back but he explained that these things happen. He said, with that kind of operation, one in ten have to be readmitted – it appeared that I had drawn the short straw. I had caught a slight infection from the catheter and I must have been prone to this because exactly the same thing had happened after my heart surgery. After a few days, things finally settled down and I was able to return home for a second time.

I was under strict instructions not to do anything but, about five days later, I had started feeling better when my grandson, Ali, dropped some YU-GI-OH cards – cards kids collect and trade – down a drain in the street. At the time YU-GI-OH was the latest craze so, of course, grandpa had to go and pull the drain cover up to retrieve them. I started bleeding again but, fortunately, it wasn't bad enough to go back into hospital. However, perhaps I would have been safer going back to the ward rather than having to face the wrath of Shirley for being so daft. She had a point.

I'd sent the consultant, Mr Meddings, a bottle of port as a thank-you for his care and a few weeks later I received a lovely letter from him. It read:

Dear Mr Devine

Just to let you know the result of the tissue that was sent away showed no evidence of anything sinister.

I hope you feel OK and thank you for your very generous present.

And I sincerely hope this isn't the last chapter in your book.

Well, this *is* the last chapter but, with luck, it won't be the last chapter in my life. Maybe I could have been a better father and husband over the years but I did the best that I could. I hope that the many fans who come to see my shows think that I have given them all that I could and they've had some fun along the way too, with, hopefully, many more great times to come.

And, on that note – 'Get the kettle on, Shirley!'